THE GREATEST LIONS

Also available by J. B. G. Thomas:

THE MEN IN SCARLET

THE ROARING LIONS

THE AVENGING ALL BLACKS

THE GREATEST LIONS

The Story of the British Lions Tour Of South Africa, 1974

J. B. G. THOMAS

With a Foreword by
WILLIE JOHN McBRIDE

PELHAM BOOKS

First published in Great Britain by Pelham Books Ltd
52 Bedford Square, London WC1B 3EF
OCTOBER 1974
SECOND IMPRESSION MARCH 1975

ISBN 0 7207 0786 2

Printed in Great Britain by
Hollen Street Press Ltd at Slough
and bound by Dorstel Press, Harlow

'To the youngest members of the Thomas family,
Jonathon and Malcolm'

CONTENTS

ILLUSTRATIONS

The author's thanks are due to the following whose copyright pictures are reproduced in this book: *Allen Lipschitz* (*1, 9*); *Gert Hattingh* (*2, 10, 15, 18*); *The Argus* (*3, 4, 7, 20*); *Rod Samson* (*5*); *Jan Nel* (*6, 16, 17, 19*); *Basil Hall* (*8, 11*); *John Rubython* (*12, 13, 14*).

PREFACE

It is customary to thank all those who helped me in the production of a tour book and as this reports the tour of the 'Greatest Lions' there are many. First, my Managing Director and Editor for sending me on tour, then the members of the Sports Staff of my paper, followed by Vivian Jenkins and several members of the press gang and two photographers, John Rubython and Gert Hattingh, who supplied me with such wonderful illustrations.

However, without the magnificent displays of the 1974 Lions, nothing would have been achieved and *all* members of the party were most cheerful and helpful, but especially Alun Thomas, Syd Millar and Willie John McBride who was kind enough to contribute the Foreword.

South African officials and friends, as always, were most helpful and 'Little Farm' proved a superb author's hideout. As this was my last long tour, I enjoyed it as much I did the previous six and it is indeed pleasant to have watched British rugby climb back to the top again. I saw my first test at Ellis Park in 1955 with a thrilling victory and this tour ended there with a thrilling draw. Indeed, I have been lucky to watch superb rugby and travel with so many friends abroad!

J. B. G. Thomas
Cardiff. August 1974

FOREWORD

by Willie John McBride
(Captain of the 1974 British Lions)

It now being over a decade since I first travelled with the Lions, and having seen many lean days of Lions rugby in those early years, it gives me the greatest pleasure to write this foreword for the author's seventh book on Lions touring.

As I've said, I saw the lean years when players dreams and hopes were shattered by defeat, I was indeed lucky to be retained and share in those happy days of 1971 in New Zealand, but naturally 1974 will always last in my memories. The Lions tour of 1974 was different – for me at least. Not only had we controversy and doubts of the tour even taking place, but I had the great honour to Captain what turned out to be the greatest team of players I've ever travelled with and what an easy job they made for me. If I were asked to describe the 1974 Lions, I think the most important fact that sticks out in my mind is that there were no stars but great men who arrived in South Africa with one purpose and that was to win. What loyalty they showed to one another and to the management – we were all one.

A major tour of this length has strains with thirty-two men living together for three months, but I will never forget the tolerance, the understanding and the will to stick at the task like this lot. Of course it was tough, but how they all, and I stress *all*, worked so enthusiastically in training and how they were rewarded on the playing field. At times I marvelled at the determination and dedication – it seemed at times when we did struggle in a game that everyone reacted to the call in unison – WE WILL NOT ACCEPT DEFEAT.

Don't be mislead by all the hard work, there were many great moments, indeed hours spent off the field and I know the comradeship built up will long remain amongst these heroes. They were great singers as well and I will never forget the coach journey to that Second Test in Pretoria – we arrived at the ground in a voice of confidence I've never before experienced and no one made a move to leave the coach until we finished the song some minutes later.

To these men, who were steadfast of purpose and who reached their goal the only way possible – through hard work – all I can simply say is THANK YOU for making my dreams a reality.

To the Manager for the part he played and to the Coach who made my job an easy one – THANK YOU.

To the author, with whom I've travelled many miles and enjoyed many chats and who always enjoyed that phrase I used so much in 1974 – NOTHING FOR THE PRESS – it was great to travel with you again.

'Willie John'

CHAPTER ONE

The Judgement

The 1974 Lions will be known as the greatest, although long may be the argument among rugby men, especially those who saw the major part of both the 1971 and 1974 tours, as to whether the 1974 side was a better one than its immediate predecessor. Having followed both tours closely and enjoyed them to the full; and after taking into account all the circumstances prevailing, one must give the 1974 side the accolade, if only by a short head. In the first place they became the first Lions side of the century to go through a major tour without defeat and suffer only one draw, and that in the very last match. They won the four match test series against South Africa by the margin of three victories and a draw to nil; something that has never been achieved before, and it did much to improve the image of British sport and maintain the high standards set by the 1971 side in New Zealand.

For efficiency and consistency there has never been a British side like this one of 1974, and, although it may not have produced the grand spectacle of the 1971 side when beating Wellington, no previous Lions side has played with such control in a test match, as did the 1974 side in the first three. The mud of Cape Town saw it produce supreme tactical control at forward and half; the firm ground and sun of Pretoria saw it achieve a record victory with running rugby, and the green grass of Port Elizabeth saw it preform as the perfect team in the second half.

One could argue that the back divisions of the 1938, 1955, 1959 and 1971 sides were often better than the 1974 side in the matter of colour and spectacle and sometimes attacking artistry. Again, one could argue that some of the test sides opposed by these touring sides down through the years were stronger than the Springboks of 1974. Indeed, all things are relative, and it is not easy to compare sides in different eras. Some would say it is too difficult, nay, dangerous but one has to place the highly successful 1974 side in its rightful place, at the head of the list, if strongly challenged by the 1971 side in second place, and 1955 and 1959 in joint third. Of the seven successive Lions sides I have followed in twenty years, this is the order of merit in which I would like to see them placed, although my judgement would be far from final, but the safest way is to compare results, which provides a fascinating exercise.

The 1955 side shared in the greatest test abroad, the 1st at Ellis Park, that produced a 23–22 result and some of the greatest attacking rugby as well as excitement against a good Springbok side; yet this side of great talent was never organised or properly coached, but was full of remarkable players. The 1959 Lions had equal ability but lacked coaching and lost out only through some simple errors and indifferent refereeing. It was often brilliant without plan and possessed some remarkable backs. The 1971 side had flair and skill and achieved amazing success to prove what coaching, organisation and good leadership can do for a British rugby team abroad. The 1974 side enjoyed the benefits of all that had gone before and with a team spirit second to none, inspired captaincy, shrewd coaching and diplomatic management, proved itself the greatest, yet it would be the first to acknowledge the fine players and matches that highlighted previous tours. Likewise, camp followers and those who listened, read and watched at home, may argue if only 'so and so' had been in the 1974 side, and so on, but any management has to make the best of the resources available and this is where the 1974 Lions deserve to win the title.

All tribute to the four Home Unions and their new attitude to Lions teams and the special preparations for long tours abroad. No one was more pleased with the team's success than John Tallent and Albert Agar, and many a day I sat with Albert Agar and John Law and said, 'Isn't it nice and a pleasant change to see a Lions side succeed overseas as did successive touring teams in the British Isles until recently!' The pendulum of power has swung and returned to the Northern Hemisphere from the Southern, where it had remained from 1903 onwards until the brave and fighting victory of the 1971 men in New Zealand. The four Home Unions have become realists; the players are now 'professional' in their approach to the game on the field, although they are still amateurs. Indeed, they must be the greatest and most successful amateur performers of all time in that their 22 matches produced 3½ million rand for South African rugby which is over £2,000,000, at a personal gain of 75p per man per day as out of pocket expenses. This is a supreme love for, and dedication to, the amateur game and one can only salute these young heroes so ably led and managed and who, despite all alleged reports to the contrary, behaved in the manner of true ambassadors, in a land where the long ties with Britain are being strained to the utmost. At least one felt at the end of the tour that South Africans can still have respect for the British and their attitude to sport and to South Africa's national game.

Their dedication and loyalty to manager, coach and captain was outstanding and there were no 'outsiders' or 'loners' in the party. Very occasionally a player over-celebrated on Saturday and Sunday but he knew all about it on Monday morning when the training session was obviously the hardest of the week. This intense devotion to the side as a whole on the part of each player produced two things, a magnificent team spirit in which the players were prepared to 'die' for their captain and follow him to the 'death', and a genuine desire to enjoy the business of winning without becoming over-elated or over-confident as the result of continued success.

The side had balance and strength in depth and it was the strength in depth, as much as the experience and skills of the top players, that made it all-powerful and produced the unbeaten record. It had been wisely selected and as much praise for this must go to Manager Alun Thomas and Coach Syd Millar as to the Four Home Unions selection committee. Several leading players were not available and in a way this was a fortuitous challenge as it made players and management all the more determined to make good their absence from the tour. Wise use was made of the material available and a devotion to training and clean play prevented the party suffering a long and serious injury list.

It is true that Alan Old, when promising to reach new heights as a player and points scorer was struck down unnecessarily when just about to blossom, and he was missed at first before Phil Bennett and Andy Irvine made good the loss. Young Irvine, following a shaky start, blossomed forth to prove himself a worthy match winner and the most improved back on the tour. Young

Clive Rees suffered a double blow and although he may not have made the test side, he was developing and was missed. Still, only two men were to really suffer, although several of the favoured backs like Roy Bergiers, Geoffrey Evans and John Moloney were out for long periods with muscle injuries and illness. Yet the experienced men survived superbly for Willie John McBride, Gareth Edwards, J. P. R. Williams, Ian McLauchlan, Mervyn Davies, Roger Uttley, Gordon Brown, Fergus Slattery and Sandy Carmichael were almost indestructible. Of these nine, eight had been through New Zealand in 1971 and the two leaders, McBride and Edwards, in South Africa in 1968. This vital experience formed the real hard core of a successful side, and there were others who played important parts in supporting roles.

The nucleus of the 1971 side was provided in five forwards; McBride, McLauchlan, Brown, Davies and Slattery, who helped form the best pack ever to leave the shores of Britain and, before the end of the tour, Danie Craven compared it with his superbly gifted 1951 Springboks pack, and Bob Scot with All Blacks of 1950, 1967 and 1969, while there were some who said that they would have held their own against the mighty Springboks of 1937. These are notable testimonials and I have not seen a better pack in action, for while solid controlled scrummaging was its basic attribute, as must be with all great packs, its domination in the tight-loose play and, until the last test, the line-out play, revealed it as one of the great packs of the century.

The front row was unusual in size and balance yet perfectly suited. McLauchlan was an ideal loose-head, even at 5 ft. 8 in., and Windsor a tough, lively hooker at 5 ft. 9 in., but Fran Cotton at tight head was 6 ft. 2 in., to suggest that such a combination had little opportunity of succeeding against taller Springbok front rows, but it did in match after match. The second row had McBride giving the complete answer to those who said he would not hold his place, apart from being a successful captain. McBride was an essential 'hard core', as in New Zealand in 1971, and a far better captain than even his friends suggested. For him it was the perfect tour with supreme dedication, honesty and great humour.

The choice of his partner fell to smiling Gordon Brown, who had graduated to the big time as a rugby player in New Zealand in 1971. He was a hard, controlled forward who developed a habit of scoring tries and finished with eight; the most by any lock on a long tour. These then were the front five; the foundation of the team and its success, and the team's main armoury. Not until the last test were the front five held, and then without Brown, and Windsor and McLauchlan were injured during the match. Behind them were three experts forming the loose trio in Mervyn Davies at No. 8, and he has never played better; Fergus Slattery who confirmed his promise shown in 1971, and Roger Uttley, the utility forward par excellence, who came into the pack as a flanker to do the job that was originally intended for Derek Quinnell, had he been fit at the time of the touring team selection. All eight, two from each of the four home countries, formed the perfect blend, the basic strength of the side.

The selectors on tour concentrated on this pack and added other things to it, although it had the trump card immediately behind this pack in Gareth Edwards, who played the best rugby of his eight year representative career and was hall-marked by South African critics as the greatest individual player in the side. They called him the King of the Lions and he was a remarkable match winner and controller; strong, accurate, efficient, tireless and, like J. P. R. Williams at full-back, a fierce competitor, who was satisfied with nothing less than victory. I have never seen Edwards produce better rugby, either for his side or himself, while his combination with Phil Bennett produced a much higher standard than it had for Wales previously, and Edwards was always happier when Bennett was in the side, since he was prone to attempt too much and try too hard when Bennett was absent. Together, they were the link men and controllers of the test side, and it was only when Bennett was physically below par with injury in the Fourth Test, and good possession was less than normal, that they did not control as effectively as in first three when they made absolutely certain that no good possession was wasted; that the points for victory were scored, and the opposition put under almost continuous pressure.

If you were to ask a South African which player he thought had worried them most in their winter of discontent, he would say Edwards and he was, in the 1974 tour, what Barry John, his former partner, was in the 1971 tour. So Edwards is the new king in his own right, and Bennett improved to such an extent as to impress even his sternest critics who said he was a kicker rather than a runner. In the Second Test he did extremely well and had he not suffered injury to his knee when scoring a superb try, he would have bloomed even more portently. His knee cartilage injury worried him considerably after the Second Test and although he played in four more matches after a break of four, he was never able to play flat out again, even though assuming a vital role in the Third Test with two dropped goals and several spirited runs aided by a pain killing injection. In all the side owed much to Bennett, the little man who, though self-effacing, had a bigger heart than he was given credit for on this tour.

Behind Bennett were two sound centres, and as the fine pair of 1971 were not available, Thomas and Millar had to develop two more. All four on tour were given a chance and while Bergiers suffered early injury and then a slight loss of accuracy through injury after-effects, he and Evans could not displace Milliken and McGeechan. It will be recalled that Milliken had played his eight internationals for Ireland in the shadow of the established Mike Gibson, but on tour he emerged as a remarkably sound industrious player and an excellent tourist and formed with McGeechan, a utility back, the happiest of partnerships in the centre. They may not have reached the peak of Dawes and Gibson at their best in 1971, or engaged in the flashing finger tip passing style, but they did all that was asked of them and a little more. Bergiers and Evans were unlucky in many ways but all four centres were friends and even when Gibson arrived, to seek his test place, the selectors kept faith with 'Dick and Ian', the established firm, for the tests and, remember, the selectors were composed of two Irishmen and one Welshman.

To complete the top three-quarter line, the selectors went for J. J. Williams, the smiling Welsh whippet, and Billy Steele, the Scottish 'dodger', who made up for his lack of overall pace in elusiveness. Williams, after a quiet start on heavy grounds, blossomed forth on the firm dry grounds of the highveld, while Steel after a rib injury lost a little of his sharpness. Rees was put out of the running through injury; Grace was a slow developer and it as not until the 15th match that saw this happy, pleasant young man with long legs, running really well. Yet there was one back who had to be included, as one of the best attackers in the side, and as Irvine had no chance of displacing J. P. R. Williams, he was placed on the right wing instead of Steele who had to miss six of the last seven matches through injury. Irvine was an 'instant' success in the test scene and became one of the best and speediest attacking backs in the side, and top points scorer with 156, ahead of Bennett with 103 in three fewer matches. J. P. R. Williams at full-back was superb and was one of the top half dozen players in the party who had a major influence upon the winning of the series. If anything, he improved upon his 1971 New Zealand form and can thus be adjudged as the greatest full-back of his decade and one of the greatest in the game. Indeed, he and Edwards were the two world class backs in the side; the two really strong, indestructable, brilliant performers.

Tactically, the 1974 Lions decided that they could win the test series if they could contain the Springboks at forward and, expecting hard forward play in the first match of the tour at Potchefstroom, they were surprised at the manner in which they won the ball, and also the way the backs handled on the dry, firm ground. Yet a touring team is always vulnerable in its early matches and this team was no exception. Many of its members were surprised at Windhoek by the vigour and loose play of South West Africa, and it is just possible that had the Free State or Northern Transvaal met the Lions in the second match of the tour, defeat could have been suffered; in the sense that strong sides like Newport (1963), and Llanelli (1972) were able to beat strong touring teams in the third and second matches respectively.

Tactically then, the itinerary favoured the Lions to some extent and for this there must be praise for Thomas and Millar plus a few friendly advisers. The first two matches gave them a touch of hard grounds after a beneficial working-up period at Stilfontein, and the decision to work up in South Africa rather than Eastbourne was a vital one. The side was well adjusted by the time it reached Cape Town, having been reminded by South West Africa that all victories would have to be earned. Great heat at Wellington was another experience and then the 'nonsense' at Port Elizabeth indicated that some sides would attempt to disturb the Lions' rhythm by attempts to rough up play.

Determined not to start anything but ready to finish any 'nonsense', the Lions wisely devised a plan that when there was need for 'retaliation' in the open it would be all or none. Thus the later occasional scenes of ten Lions wading in, and especially in the Third Test, reflected the 'new look' in British touring rugby, as they would not be intimidated. The message got round and the Lions held firm to their captain's decree, 'There is no escape. We will take no prisoners!' In the past, Lions teams have taken a great deal, as sportsman, and not retaliated, and although I do not condone rough play, whatever the provocation, I do believe the 1974 Lions were right in this and have set a pattern for the future. It served a useful purpose since such 'incidents' were short and sharp, and there were few if any matches other than that against the Eastern Province where there was persistent niggling. A couple of good blows were landed at Port Elizabeth, yet where trouble was anticipated, there was none.

Rugby Football is not particularly rough or dirty in South Africa and, in most instances, as can be said of rugby everywhere, it does depend upon referees, whose task grows harder with the passing of each year. If referees go in 'hard' early on when there is rough play and look for the 'offending' players, and not only those poor fellows seen to be 'retaliating', then much more can be achieved, although referees as a body are still reluctant to send off important 'offenders' since Unions do not favour the officials after such strong administration of justice.

Again, the tour indicated the need for neutral referees to relieve the burden of those officials having to referee matches in which their own countries are engaged. It is never an easy task and a referee has to live with his decision and errors, however unintentional, should his own country lose. Refereeing does play an important part, and did in this tour, as in New Zealand in 1971. The Lions had Max Baise at Cape Town and because he was out of favour with the South African Board and was experienced they thought he would do well. There were no complaints, certainly not from the Lions.

Then, for the Second Test, the Lions chose Cas de Bruyn, who had not had a good match at Windhoek, and Syd Millar, who studied all referees closely, decided de Bruyn would have a much better match in a test. He got the job; did well, and was selected for the Third and, again, he satisfied the Lions, even though there were 'punch-ups'. How could he have sent off ten or more players? The Lions altogether '99' plan for emergency action made it impossible for referees to send off players but it also cooled the opposition.

When it came to the last test, the Lions could not have de

Bruyn again, but they recalled certain cases in the past when referees changed their approach. However, they felt that Baise would be reasonable again as the Lions had reinstated him in the International scene. He had the Fourth Test and was tense before and during since he was a Capetonian on Ellis Park, and one would not say that deep down there was any great love lost between North and South in the game in South Africa. Referees like to take charge of big matches and there are a few who will develop in South Africa, like Steve Strydom of the Free State, but one does not expect any section of any crowd to treat a referee as the Ellis Park boo-boys treated Ian Gourlay of Natal during and after the Quaggas match. That was stupid and unkind even if he did make mistakes.

On the whole, I feel the Lions have no real grouse against South African referees, for although mistakes were made, they appeared to even out. Max Baise made mistakes in the Fourth Test which the Lions could just have won, as Slattery appears to have scored, but a draw was a just result on the day. By the next long tour, there could be neutral referees in the Southern Hemisphere, and this is long overdue, for sides would be happier whatever errors were made by neutral referees. The cost would be miminal and the Four Home Unions would welcome referees from South Africa and New Zealand for home internationals, while the whole process would lead to more uniformed interpretation of the laws.

This time in South Africa, the set scrummage and hooking laws were not pressed home to the full and the 'swinging-footed' hooker was prominent, so much so that the Lions put the ball in when the opposing hooker was at the top of his premature swing so that he would not be able to strike for the ball as his leg would have fallen by the time the ball reached the Lions hooker. Again, in the front row, McLauchlan at loose-head proved a stumbling block to most opponents and often the Lions front row was so low that the hooker, especially Windsor, frequently struck with his head! Kennedy was an experienced and quick striker and like several other members of the party unlucky not to be in the test side as, in a normal Lions side, he would have made it, but the test pack selected was extra special. Neither Windsor or Kennedy lost many tight-head strikes.

The perfect balance of the pack; in binding and positioning of feet, plus the driving over the ball followed by the pause and 'holding' when required, produced a high standard of scrummaging. The eight man shove on their opponent's 'put in' was most effective and it was real treat to see the Lions pack, low and straight as a table, with every member telling me how comfortable he felt in his job! I do believe all eight of them improved and Millar's insistence on a fine scrummaging unit in all matches was the secret and foundation of the wonderful tour record. It starts and ends with scrummaging at forward, especially in South Africa, and although some Lions forwards were less powerful scrummagers than others, the standard all round was the highest yet produced by a British touring side. The Lions found the line-out no better and no worse than in any other country, even though some referees made great play of ensuring a good gap between the two lines of forwards, as the normal infringements persisted.

Forward play throughout the world has become faster and more sophisticated, and especially so in the British Isles, where techniques have been studied and developed to a higher degree than in other countries, causing Dr Danie Craven, quite wisely, to ask that South African players in all grades apply their thoughts and energies to better scrummaging. One recalls the 1971 front row causing New Zealand provincial sides' props to 'shoot into the air' occasionally, and so the overall development in British scrummaging is a revolution and we must now expect the other countries to make an effort to catch up quickly.

Yet it was in the tight-loose play that the Lions succeeded, and where they won a great deal of ball and controlled play. In years gone by the Lions were 'killers' of the ball and now they are 'seekers', and so they win much more good ball and suffer less injury at forward. They have mastered the art of rucking and mauling, and the driving of the 1974 side at the rucks was even more impressive than that of 1971. The low binding and steady thrust plus the control of the ball as it came back, made life so much easier for Gareth Edwards or John Moloney at scrum-half. Mervyn Davies at number eight was a superb technician and he played a vital part with Edwards in the tactical controlling and link work, especially in the tests.

By the fourth test match, the Springboks had launched counter methods and thus it was much harder for a tiring Lions side, but even then, through their supreme fitness and dedication, the Lions came back in the closing stages to almost snatch the match out of the fire. Training at all times was hard and no one was spared, not even following 'heavy' week-end celebrations, and that is how it should be with any touring team. Matches are won on the practice grounds through the right coaching and interesting training. These 1974 Lions were a side, a complete unit, and they made teamwork their real spearhead.

They knew each other's job and how it was carried out. They were one for all and all for one, and the friendly relationship with no 'outsiders' in the party was as warm off the field as it was on. Again, the management specialised in its various task and then linked for regular discussions and so there were not many stones left unturned before the end of the tour. The organisation of the party eliminated much that had hampered previous tours and one believed that the political situation at home and in South Africa did much to unite the side.

The Western Province match was an important one since it appeared to mislead the Springboks selectors at the same time as it finally decided in the minds of the Lions selectors what the composition of their test side would be and, as it turned out, the Lions took no risk, and played their strongest side while the Springboks built their side round the Western Province team that had run at the Lions and scored two good tries, which incidentally was the last occasion on a Saturday for the Lions to have a try registered against them until the fourth test match!

When the First Test was played the ground was heavy and the Western Province style Springbok side was not able to run with the ball and attempted little, while the Lions set out to control it at forward and half-back. This was the most important victory, tactically, of the tour, since it disturbed the Springboks selectorial policy when they were struggling hard to build a side. It revealed the Lions forwards as a strong pack; one that would not be matched easily, but then followed the match against the Transvaal, which also misled the Springboks selectors, for with a Lions side suffering from flu and the altitude, and without key man Gareth Edwards, well though Moloney played, the Lions did not appear as strong on the highveld as it was believed they should be.

The Springboks side was changed and highveld players introduced, including the kicking Gerald Bosch at outside-half, but the situation remained unchanged as the Lions controlled the play at forward, on the hard ground, to prove themselves the complete side and so the Second Test victory at Pretoria really became the highlight of the tour in terms of playing standards. The Lions look a great side, complete in every department, at forward and behind, winning the match by twenty-eight points to nine, which was a record victory for the Lions and the largest defeat inflicted upon South Africa at home or abroad. It was halfway through the tour, and a danger point, since all sides appear to fall away at this stage. The Lions suffered a difficult week but one that requires adequate explanation as there was relaxation in a visit to the Kruger National Park immediately after the test, and the team returned to Johannesburg for a Thursday match against a strong Quaggas side and a Saturday match in Bloemfontein against a strong Free State side that was the best coached province in South Africa, thanks to Nelie Smith and Sakkie van Zyl.

For once the Lions were unprepared for a hard match. The Quaggas, with a much stronger side than was first intended, played extremely well, and the Lions just got home with the crowd having doubts about the last try that clinched the match. By this time all South Africa wanted to see the Lions beaten and every match became harder, and it was felt that if the record run of success could be halted then it would provide some encouragement for the Springboks to save the series. At Bloemfontein, the Free State played their hearts out in a bid for success and it was a damned close run thing!

Only in injury time did the Lions make a super effort to score a special try through J. J. Williams and snatch the match out of the fire, and there remained one more hard match before the Third Test. This was against the Northern Transvaal at Pretoria where the forward struggle was stern and rugged, although the Northerns won a great deal of ball and disturbed the Lions, their backs were not good enough, and their tactical kicking poor. Again, the Lions pulled out all the stops in the closing stages, as befitting a team with character and guts, and won the match 16–12. After this no one really believed that the Lions would lose.

The Third Test at Port Elizabeth was the decider and a much revised Springbok side was chosen, but without John Williams, their' best line-out forward. The Lions noted this but believed that however hard the Springboks would try and however vigorously they approached the match, they would not win it. There was a special determination and dedication about the Lions and they made only one change, Irvine for Steele on the right wing. Perfectly blended, well-drilled, confident and ready, they entered the match seeking to become the champions of the world, and after a stern first half, they did just that with a brilliant second half, in which they revealed all their best qualities. The series was won! It was, virtually, all over, and while several of the players would have left for home then, fearing an anti-climax, there were four matches still to play before they could fly out, and the scene demanded that they remained unbeaten if they were to fly home as the 'Greatest' and enjoy the high junketing through the winter, as had happened in 1971. The challenge was still on, and the Springboks were preparing for a mighty effort in the final test.

Border spoiled bravely while Natal put up a tremendously tenacious struggle before being worn down and then collapsing in injury time, while the Eastern Transvaal, contrary to expectations, provided one of the cleanest and most enjoyable matches of the tour. Came the Fourth Test with the Springboks producing their best side based on a good pack and better backs, although the continued absence of the leading scrum-half Roy McCallum, was still a blow. For the Lions it was an important match, and they had to take the field without Gordon Brown, a key forward, and the strain of the long tour and unbeaten record was beginning to tell. Again, only one Lions side since the War had won the last test of a series, in 1959 at Auckland.

They survived with a draw, and retained their unbeaten record. They became the greatest Lions and the champagne rugby of 1955 and 1959 had given way to more controlled and highly organised play. Each man played his part in the team and the concentrated effort was greater than that of the brilliant individuals of the more spectacular days. We all admired the All Blacks of 1924 but British rugby did not seek to adopt their approach, as it was too dedicated but amazingly successful. That was 50 years ago. Now in 1974 the Lions produced their special approach and high standard of efficiency and remained unbeaten for the first time since 1891. One cannot have the penny and the bun, and it has to be entertainment or success and yet I feel this

1974 side entertained extremely well and never better than in the first three tests.

It visited South Africa despite political pressure and total disownment by its government. It went to play rugby and did just that. It attracted record crowds and gate takings. It offended very few and made many friends along the way. It did a noble job for British rugby and may have eased the situation in South Africa where merit selection is on the way. It produced dedication on and off the field, but did not stifle flair, and it contained its fair share of characters. It did not lose its head and become disturbed by success. I liked this team; they were friends, and I admired its play. After twenty years of travel and seven successive Lions tours, I have witnessed changes in attitude, preparation and policy, but I have seen British Rugby become stronger and more effective. If has always been a pleasure, if often hard work, but I would not change a moment of it. Totsiens to South Africa and to long tours! There is a time and place to step down, and I have seen the Lions, in 1971 and 1974, become the 'Greatest' and that is reward enough. The game goes on!

Above: The first try of the tour. Scottish Lock Gordon Brown dives over the line in the match against Western Transvaal at Potchefstroom (*Allen Lipschitz*).

Below: The Lions team that won the first two tests. Back row, from left: Bennett, Slattery, J. P. R. Williams, McBride, Uttley, Davies, Cotton. Front row, from left: Brown, Windsor McLauchlan, Edwards, McGeechan, Steele, Milliken, J. J. Williams. Steele was replaced by Irvine in the 3rd and 4th tests. and Brown by Ralston in the 4th test (*Gert Hattingh, Die Transvaler*).

Above: Lions *v.* Protea
4th June. As Fergus
Slattery feeds the ball
from a ruck Fran Cottor
administers a right cross
to one of the Proteas'
forwards. No side
intimidated the Lions!
(*The Argus*).

Left: the 1st test at Cap
Town, 8th June.
Springbok flanker Jan
Ellis is brought down by
Slattery, with Brown,
Cotton and McLauchlan
in support (*The Argus*).

CHAPTER TWO

The Invincibles

All tours are different and even after twenty years of recording the triumphs and disasters of Lions tours, to live with a party of thirty players and their management remains an exciting adventure. The approach and attitude of teams changes with each succeeding tour and now Lions tours have an air of pleasant 'professionalism' that makes the activities all the more efficient but no less enjoyable. Again, the following of winning sides, as in 1971 and 1974, makes life much easier if harder, since there is much more to write about and one's papers become all the more demanding. Therefore, one is committed much more to one's hotel room in front of a typewriter or telephone, seven days a week, from 8.00 am to midnight. Not unpleasant work, certainly not, but a task from which there is no escape, and much of the fun that is enjoyed by the Lions and their friends cannot be shared frequently with those camp followers committed to telling the world and recording the details and highlights.

My creed is that the players' private lives should remain their own, as much as my own is my own and if, occasionally, an odd glass or chair is broken and the damage made good by immediate payment, then I do not think it requires headlines. There is a creed for rugby men and if the press are allowed the privileges of travelling with the team and enjoying its confidence, then no matter what paper, national or provincial, or those of the host country it should respect the creed and ask its representatives to live by it on tour. Occasionally, the odd 'sniper' gets to work and circulates a half truth, and generally in South Africa they come from the delightful, friendly and rather sleepy coastal town of East London!

There is always pleanty to write about, seven days a week, and the management, captain and players on this 1974 tour were always most co-operative and helpful to the press. I much enjoyed their company, all of them, and valued their friendship and, as ambassadors at large, they did Britain proud. They were as active as all fit young man; they ate well and a few of them drank well, but no more than any normal young man in his twenties who has achieved fame in sport. In fact they were far more dedicated than any previous British side in South Africa, and they would not have achieved such an honourable and impressive record had they not dedicated themselves to the task, their captain and the management.

The manager was *Alun Gruffyd Thomas*, the 48-year-old Swansea sales manager of a family business, and a district representative and former Welsh Rugby Union selector. An international utility back, he was capped 13 times for Wales, and as a 1955 Lion, was robbed of a test place through illness and injury. He was also assistant manager of the 1964 Welsh team in South Africa; a knowledgable administrator, a devotee of the cult of coaching and a friendly person in the inner circles of the game, while a happy, devoted family man. Thus he had the qualifications for managership and it was a wise appointment.

As Dr Danie Craven, and they come no wiser in the game, said at the end of the tour, Alun Thomas was the perfect manager and diplomat who never put a foot wrong. How true, even when occasionally he read the 'riot act' to his party as he was doing so to ensure that the 'image' of the party of which he was so proud would not be damaged. Once, after a test victory, at one o'clock in the morning, a British official asked him why the Lions were not perfectly dressed with collars and ties! Even he, as honorary manager and supremo was under observation, and like an admiral he had to ensure that the men under his command were made aware of what it means to be a British Lion representing one's country.

The 1974 side, following the 'adventures' of the 1968 side, were under scrutiny from their hosts and Thomas had received a stern brief about the behaviour of the team and what was expected of him and his fellows. This was a tour that had to succeed off the field as well as on and a large share of the success achieved was due to Alun Thomas. Not all members of the Press appreciated this at the time but now I feel, as they bask a little in the reflected glory of the tour, they will realise that a little 'discipline' from time to time is very necessary. If anyone thinks a tour is just one grand party then they are totally wrong, and Alun Thomas devoted many, many hours of his time to small things which may have appeared unnecessary at the time, but he cared, and the small things, as well as the big things, were important and like Doug Smith in 1971, although in a different way, succeeded. The three men 'at the top', Thomas, Millar and McBride, were an ideal partnership, although each of them was quite different as an individual, yet all three impressive as a group. Again, this tour, as that of 1971, emphasised one salient factor, a vital factor; one that helped so much to bring about success, as no tour can succeed unless the coach and the captain are 'blood brothers' of the same nationality. First, we had Dawson and Kiernan in 1968 and they did much pioneering work; then the successful James-Dawes combination, before the Millar-McBride pairing.

Coach *Sydney Millar,* the 40-year-old business executive from Ballymena, is one of post-war rugby's great characters and a big, happy man who had made three Lions tours, played in nine tests and won 37 caps for Ireland, which is an impressive record. It was his fourth visit to South Africa, and his last appearance for Ireland was in 1970, while he took over from Ronnie Dawson as coach to the Irish team in 1972, so that he was extremely well acquainted with the modern game, tactically; old enough for the players to respect him, and still fit enough to run with them. He was an ideal choice, and had played for many a season in the Irish team with the Lion's captain, McBride, which suggested there could not have been a better partnership.

As Alun Thomas told me many times on tour, it was the strong bond between Millar and McBride that won the respect of the team and was the reason why the players were ready to 'die' for these two fine Ulstermen who deeply loved their rugby and who left their homes in difficult circumstances to help a British Isles side achieve an impossible dream. Thomas never spoke other than highly of these two and he felt that Syd had a 'wonderful way with him', and was able to get the maximum out of his players on the practice field. He made them first believe in themselves and then got them to get the basics right. The next task was to get them, any 15 of them, to play as a team and although the best XV had to appear, and did appear in the tests, he discouraged and succeeded in preventing the existence of a Wednesday and a Saturday side. All the players were treated fairly and given equal opportunity.

Again, Millar studied his opponents as well as his own players. He analysed closely the approach of South African sides and their reaction to different situations. He probed their weakness and, above all, worked for 'control' and once he got his forwards and halves to control, he knew in his heart that not only would they win, but remain unbeaten. Yet he was a modest man, and never boasted of himself or his team although he defended them sternly. Little did South Africans know that this man was studying them closely, and especially their referees, and using every item of knowledge gained for the benefit of his own side. Yet he was an honest man, especially when talking to the press, of either country. He was strong and fearless, yet humble and often shy, but one hundred per cent plus in his loyalty to his friend Willie and his team. His ways were different from those of Carwyn James, the successful tactical brain of the 1971 side, but he was equally successful and efficient. Each used the particular strengths of their sides to the full, as befits an expert coach.

The dedicated, happy, big fellow, *William John McBride*, the Belfast banker, who celebrated his 34th birthday on tour, was a magnificent success in every way as captain. Of this there is no doubt; even exceeding the hopes and forecasts of those, like myself, who knew he could do the job well. He was an instant and lasting success and grew in stature, if that were possible, on this tour to leave the field at the end of the Fourth Test and say to me in the shadows of the darkened Ellis Park Stand, 'Mission accomplished. It's all history now!'

There were some who did not think that McBride would retain his place through the tour and remain the first choice lock in all four tests. He did more. He was the real 'hard core' of the best Lions pack that has ever left the shores of the British Isles for the Southern Hemisphere, and he returned a hero in every way. One cannot fault him because he had all the qualities that mattered, and a character and nature to match, a determintion that was matched by a welcome modesty, a charming smile that disarmed all so easily, and a rugby enthusiasm that will not be easily matched.

He stood like a mountain among his fellows and his team were ready to 'die' for him. When he went down in the last scrum at

Bloemfontein he said, 'Gentlemen, this team has character and guts. Let us show them that we have, and win this last scrum!' His appeal was simple and straightforward, and he led by example, while a nod here, a tap there and a little word now and again kept his men with him as would a hen with her new born chicks. Yet he inspired confidence and vigour while always believing that rugby was a hard game. He was never a dirty player at any time in his long career as the most capped of rugby players with 57 Irish caps and 17 test appearances, both records.

His tour belief was, 'There is no escape. We will take no prisoners,' when playing, and off the field he would say 'I go in search of wisdom!' There will always be a place for McBride in the game in any country as he is loved, respected and admired, and he faced his greatest challenge, the 1974 leadership, with a dedication that surprised all who knew him well. On suddenly being given the pack leadership when Ray McLoughlin was injured in 1971, he girded his loins for battle and slotted in to the task quite easily, and revealed then that he was the obvious choice for the 1974 leadership because he did not believe in failure through lack of effort. Like Millar, a true man's man from Ballymena; he was a gentle family man, and perhaps it was his love of people, sense of duty, and a respect for tolerance which, when added to his considerable rugby skill, made him a great and respected leader.

Full-back *John Peter Rhys Williams* was a remarkable player and competitor and, at 25 years of age, the outstanding player in his position in the world. So good in fact as to draw acclamation from as wise a judge as Ace Parker, who commented that Williams was the best full-back he had seen. Fearless, strong, accurate and blessed with pace, he looked at all times the ideal player in his position and was immaculately consistent, but especially so in the tests. He made 15 appearances and scored three tries. Recently qualified as a doctor, he stayed on in South Africa.

Full-back and utility player *Andrew Robertson Irvine* was the most improved young player in the side, and one who now has a brilliant future before him that must warm the hearts of all former pupils of Heriot's, if not all Scots. A pleasant, eager young player, he started nervously, but gathered confidence and became one of the most exciting backs and prolific scorers in the side. He forced his way into the test side on the wing, and appeared in the 3rd and 4th, while his tally of 156 points is the highest scored by a Lion in South Africa. Irvine has all the pace and skill of a three-quarter but prefers to remain an attacking full-back. An excellent tourist who proved there is nothing really wrong with modern students. Made 15 appearances.

The dapper wing *John James Williams* became known as 'J.J.' and grew in stature as the tour progressed because of his remarkable strides as a player and try scorer, especially in the important matches. He made 12 appearances, including all four tests, and scored six tries at Mossel Bay to equal the Lions record and create a new one in South Africa. In 2nd and 3rd Tests he scored two spanking tries in each and on the hard ground earned the title of the 'Welsh Whippet' from his fellows. Happy, cheerful and an interested tourist who ran splendidly and elusively, and one who learned much from the tour while establishing himself as a test wing of quality. A schoolmaster (P.E.).

The singing Scottish wing *William Charles Common Steel*e was a quiet, effective player who appeared in the first two tests before suffering rib injuries that allowed him to play only three more matches and miss the last two tests. Yet he was a worker and collected seven tries in nine matches as well as being an able defender. He loved the ballads of Scotland and sang them well and behaved as one would expect an RAF NCO, with dignity and loyalty. He regarded it as a privilege and a pleasure to tour, but feels that all his career he must be plagued with injuries, yet he reached the top on this tour and made the test side on merit.

The tall, dashing Irish wing and accountant *Thomas Oliver Grace* took a long time to come to the boil and then one could not stop him racing for the line, to finish as top try scorer with 13 in 11 matches, one ahead of J.J., which gave the Irishman much pleasure as they were friendly rivals. A happy, excellent tourist and one of Ned's faithful church party, he was a kind, wholehearted character who enjoyed chatting with all and sundry and made sure that people liked the Lions. Will obviously enjoy himself on and off the field during the Ireland Centenary as a real rugby man.

Clive Frederick Williams Rees, next to Alan Old, was the unluckiest member of the side as he broke a bone in his hand, recovered, and then fractured the same bone again, thus proving that lightning does strike twice in the same place. He left the party after the third test in accordance with the tour agreement, but he accepted his misfortune in a quiet manner and was a faithful member of the party. Chosen because club mate Gerald Davies could not travel, he learned much on tour in six appearances that should help him with Wales in furture. At 22 he was actually the fifth Llanelli player in the side although playing for the London Welsh.

Gerald Davies was requested to replace Rees, but could not travel and *Alan John Morley* of Bristol flew out to play in two matches and return to his Bristol club as a full Lion, and no club deserved the honour more. He was well built and a strong runner, and should retain his place in the England side, while he learned much about touring in the few weeks he was in South Africa, sitting quietly in the background.

After living in the shadow of an outstanding Lion centre, Mike Gibson, a fellow Ulsterman, *Richard Alexander Milliken* accepted readily the opportunity to prove himself a fine and reliable test centre, appearing in all four tests, playing consistently and making total of 13 appearances with five tries. A happy, contented tourist whose winning smile disarmed all and sundry, and who was a real entertainer when he put his mind to it. With McGeechan he formed a sound partnership and, as a pair, they had much to do with the total of ten tries scored in the tests. A strong runner with a good hand off, he showed his special skills in the Transvaal match.

With Milliken was the shrewd Yorkshire born Scot, *Ian Robert McGeechan,* whose bright eyes indicated his alertness and general usefulness on the field of play. Little escaped him and in many ways he was a replica as a player of manager Alun Thomas. He had played at centre and outside-half for Scotland and did the same duty for Lions in 14 appearances. Unselfish in approach, he had to wait until the penultimate match to record his first try of the tour but collected an excellent dropped goal in the Second Test. Another loyal and contented tourist.

There were high hopes that *Roy Thomas Edmond Bergiers,* the Llanelli centre, would make the test side and he started extremely well in the first match but was injured towards the end of it and his damaged rib muscles were a long time repairing, and although he played after a short rest he then suffered illness in midtour which kept him out of five successive matches. Thus he was never able to fully challenge the men in possession but accepted his misfortune with good grace and enjoyed his tour. Known as 'Budgy', he was a prolific letter writer, although hotly challenged by Bennett and J.J. He made nine appearances and learned much that should help him with Wales.

England's sharp-moving centre *Geoffrey William Evans* was a 'martyr' to hamstring trouble after promising much in the early matches. An ideal build for his position and possessing speed off the mark, he too was unlucky and when any player is injured on tour, he is automatically out of the side and cannot challenge. The rivalry is keen, if friendly, and Evans, who had played well for England and Coventry, was expected to get close to test side even without his pacy club partner, Peter Preece. He made eight appearances and scored four tries.

When Alan Old was injured, by a late tackle in the Proteas match, *Cameron Michael Henderson Gibson,* was requested to to travel as he had intimated that he would be available towards the end of June as a late replacement. Before the tour started he was an automatic choice for the test side but after watching the Second Test on arrival, he was unable to displace Milliken and McGeechan in the last two tests, although he served the side well in seven out of a possible ten matches. With three Lions tours behind him he was a most experienced player but accepted his fate readily and enjoyed his 'short' tour at 31 years of age.

The dynamic little Welsh outside-half, *Phillip Bennett,* built up his form steadily after a brilliant first match display at Potchefstroom and was the 'star' of the Second Test match, scoring a superb try but, in doing so, injured a knee cartilage and instep. He then missed four matches and played in four of the last six when he was virtually 'walking wounded'. Yet his spirit was splendid as was his eagerness to play despite no obvious delight at training! In 11 appearances including four tests he scored 103 points and when in harness with Edwards formed a superb pair of controllers. He played his best rugby as an attacker in the top class on tour and his kicking was superb.

The saddest injury on the tour was that suffered by England's outside-half *Alan Gerald Bernard Old* who was keen to play in a test match while his brother was playing cricket for England, but a late tackle in the Proteas match tore a ligament in his left knee and he had to be operated upon the next day. He took it all with typical Yorkshire grit and after chatting to him in hospital my admiration increased one hundred per cent. All the Lions crammed into his small single ward before they left Cape Town and sang to him after opening the champagne. He had created a new Lions individual points scoring record with 37 at Mossel Bay and for this alone he will long be remembered as a fine player and worthy Lion, although he intends to play again for at least another year.

Without doubt the most powerful and successful individual player of the tour was *Gareth Owen Edwards*, the outstanding Cardiff and Wales scrum-half who, with J. P. R. Williams, gave real strength and control to the back division. Playing in his third Lions tour he achieved greater success than ever before and set himself new standards while adding a new dimension to scrum-half play. Much feared by the Springboks, who attempted to mark him closely yet found him to be, continually, a match winner of skill, daring and determination. South Africa believed him to be the world's best scrum-half at the start of the tour, and from the first match at Potchefstroom where he substituted for an injured John Moloney, he held the scene whenever he was in action. He played exceedingly well with Bennett as a pair of tactical controllers although occasionally he attempted to do rather too much when without his Welsh partner. Made 15 appearances including all four tests and scored seven tries and a dropped goal.

The likeable young Irishman, *John Joseph Moloney*, who suffered a dislocation of his shoulder in the first match of the tour, recovered quickly and proved an able deputy to Edwards, even though he suffered hamstring trouble towards the end. A quiet, efficient player with a good service and excellent break from set pieces, he was man enough to admit that he learned much from watching Edwards in action. A ready, dry turn of wit, he was 'brother' of Ned the 'Times' and the pair of them held many an interesting conversation over a cup of tea. Moloney was much liked and respected and as a young Dublin businessman proved an ideal tourist, making eight appearances and scoring three tries.

The hooking test place went to the 26-year-old Welshman, *Robert William Windsor*, known as the 'Duke', of the famous Pontypool Club, who had also played for Cross Keys and Cardiff, and was in his first year as an international, having succeeded former Lion Jeff Young in the Welsh side. He just beat the more experienced Ken Kennedy into the position and became one of the 'characters' of the team. His ready wit and keen sense of humour enabled him to assume the role which his club coach, Ray Prosser, performed on the 1959 tour. Admits to learning great deal from Ian McLauchlan and to occasionally hooking with his head in the 'anything goes' South African scrums. Made 12 appearances including four tests, and almost qualified for a fireman's helmet as did his coach in 1962.

The senior medical officer in the party was Ireland's most capped hooker *Kenneth William Kennedy,* a 1966 Lion, who did a splendid job on and off the field and many were the players and pressmen he attended during the tour, and he is deserving of their thanks. He became engaged on tour to attractive Shelley Latham, Miss South Africa 1973, and the team shared in the celebration party after the Northern Transvaal match at Pretoria. No matter the time, day or night, a call to Ken would always ensure first class medical attention and his efforts were warmly praised by Manager Thomas. On the field he made ten appearances, playing with his traditional enthusiasm, talking to all and sundry, including referees and touch judges, but was a splendid tourist.

The most amazing forward in the side was *John 'Mighty Mouse' McLauchlan* of Scotland, his country's captain and successful 'veteran' of the 1971 tour. At 32 years of age, and 5 ft 8 in and 15 st, he gave all tight-head props in South Africa a lesson in scrummaging and it was only in the last match of the tour that his efficiency was reduced as result of deep thigh bruising early on. He made 13 appearances including four tests and led the side against Southern Universities. Most knowledgable and loyal tourist as well as a keen tactical student of game, and yet enjoyed the life off the field with good humour, developing a close personal friendship with Windsor, teaching the Welshman much about the 'mysteries' of front row play. Like Edwards of Wales, he was the reigning Scottish captain.

His Scottish prop colleague was the tight-head West of Scotland 30-year-old *Alexander Bennett Carmichael,* who was called 'Sandy' when 'ABC' would have been easier, but another splendid tourist. Missed tests in New Zealand through injury and just pipped on this tour by England's Fran Cotton, but he never complained after 35 caps for Scotland. He was prepared to play loose or his specialist tight-head and was a lively, happy tourist who set an example in loyalty to younger players.

Many a campaigner has taken such disappointment to 'heart' but Carmichael, probably the cleanest and most sporting representative forward of the decade, preferred to enjoy his rugby. Scotland will need him, until he choses to retire, packing down with McLauchlan. Enjoyed conversations with Vivian Jenkins about dogs and bag packing.

The strong young man from Rugby League country, *Frances Edward Cotton*, on his first Lions tour, after visiting Japan, South Africa and New Zealand in successive years with England, did well to win the tight-head prop place in the first test and played well enough to retain it. A PE master, he was fit and hard, but an extremely pleasant tourist with the determination of the North deep in his bones. He learned much on tour and was a specialist in 'T' shirts, but earned fame off the field for his ability to sleep anywhere at anytime. Made 14 appearances including all four tests and led the side in the cliff-hanger against Quaggas. Received regular telegrams from home.

Gloucester's contribution to the side was the bluff, big hearted *Michael Alan Burton*, the burly 28-year-old England tight-head who kept challenging colleague Cotton in his own country. He suffered an ankle injury and then a most painful eye injury that allowed him only three appearances in the first 12 matches. Yet with considerable medical aid from Dr Kennedy and his own spirit, he played in five of the last ten matches and regained his form. An amusing 'character', he shared with Windsor the honour of the 'clown prince' and enlivened many a long journey. Proud of Gloucester and England, he was an unlucky player but a good companion.

Few tourists in recent years, except myself as a non-player have been habitual cigar smokers but I found a rival on tour in *Christopher Wayne Ralston* of Richmond and England. Given the name of 'Lurch' by his team-mates, one rarely found him without a small cigar, and although he was a comparatively silent tourist he enjoyed himself and allowed himself a moment of animation when selected for the last test with an extra cigar! He worked hard on the field but was unlucky with injury and suffered a painful tooth abscess followed by a KO and cracked cheek in the Leopards match. Yet it is to his credit that he rarely complained.

Toured Japan, South Africa and New Zealand with England before this his first Lions tour, and was the tallest man in the team at 6 ft 6 in. Made 13 appearances.

A powerful lock who was prevented from appearing in all four tests as he missed the last through injury was *Gordon Lamont Brown,* a direct descendant from Dr Livingstone who opened up Africa for the Lions many years before! A big powerful lock, he reached his peak on this tour after promising to do so in New Zealand in 1971. Member of a famous Scottish sporting family, although brother Peter never became a Lion, Gordon has an infectious sense of humour and apart from making 14 appearances he created a new record for a lock forward on tour with eight tries, and achieved his ambition of playing a round of golf with Gary Player, plus team-mates Edwards and Gibson. Carried a Springbok head round South Africa.

One of the most consistent players in the party and blessed with ideal temperament for the tour was Englishman *Roger Miles Uttley* who, at 24, can still become the best utility forward in the game or one of England's most remembered locks. Strong, tall and quick about the field, he has big hands and is ideally suited to the modern game, especially on the flank where he assumed the role intended for Quinnell. A North country man, he had grit and determination, and registered his only try in final test but enjoyed it all very much. Blessed with a big cheery face he smiled his way through the tour as an excellent ambassador.

Ireland's *John Fergus Slattery* was actually selected for the third test in 1971 but had to withdraw through illness only to advance considerably in three years and make the flank position his own on this tour, playing with outstanding efficiency and aggressiveness, as well as proving a lively entertainments secretary off the field. As befitting an auctioneer, he was a fast talker but enjoyed the tour to the full, and maintained close contact with the press. Made 12 appearances, scored six tries, and twice captained the team to suggest that he could well succeed eventually the magnificent McBride as captain of Ireland.

Ulster's flanker *Stewart Alexander McKinney* had long spells of injury but made eight appearances and his one score, a penalty against the Free State, the only match in which he place kicked, was a vital factor in the two point victory. A strong, cheerful flanker, he had few opportunities of challenging Slattery and

Uttley because of injury, but battled away and landed the best left hook of the tour on a miscreant Eastern Province player at Port Elizabeth. Enjoyed the tour on and off the field in the traditional manner of his countrymen and should win more caps for Ireland.

The fiery Welshman *Thomas Patrick David* started the tour like an express train and appeared in the first three matches, driving and mauling with the best but then pulled a hamstring against Boland and never quite recovered his best form. By then the test places had gone to Slattery and Uttley and he was disappointed but, like Ripley, he was an excellent driver and runner but not too expert at distribution, and one feels that he yet may make a better international prop than he is a flanker. Visited New Zealand in 1971 at his own expense and decided he would become a Lion.

Perhaps the most disappointed player at not winning a test place was England's fine active flanker *Anthony Neary,* who had made 22 consecutive appearances for England and helped his country beat South Africa and New Zealand on tour. Has a fine sense of position, good hands and plenty of pace and it was always a close struggle between Slattery and himself. However, an excellent and handsome tourist, he gave of his best at all times and quickly recovered from the test disappointment. A solicitor, he was 25 on tour and should add many more caps to his name.

Another player (and one of six English forwards in the side) who wanted to make the test side was *Anthony George Ripley* who had won 16 caps for his country at No. 8. He was good on the charge and lively in the loose scoring five tries, but not quite the defensive technician that Mervyn Davies proved to be on his second successive Lions tour. Yet Ripley was popular with the crowds, and for the unconventional clothes that he wore, especially his native sandals and wide variety of 'T' shirts. Quick witted, intelligent and lively, if a trifle non-conformist, he appeared to enjoy tour to the full. Extremely fond of taped jazz.

Finally, the immaculate, tall Welsh No. 8 *Thomas Mervyn Davies,* who must have smoked more cigarettes than Ralston and myself did cigars, but was a tremendous worker on the field, earning the accolade of the best No. 8 in the world. Was shaken by his first appearance at Windhoek but after that never looked back and became the 'Merve the Swerve' of his best days, with consistent form at line-out and scrum, and in the loose, working in close harmony with Edwards as link man between the backs and forwards. Has 26 caps for Wales and eight test appearances but says it was his last Lions tour, although New Zealand may still beckon in 1977. Wore old camouflaged army hat and made 12 appearances with five tries.

Representing the South African Board and 'mothering' the whole party as chief liaison officer was a kindly official, Choet Visser of Bloemfontein, who was most experienced in his task and helped enormously to keep the 'show on the road'. A wealthy business man, he was generous and kind, and a real rugby fanatic while his charming wife also helped the party in several ways, not least as a hostess at two superb parties held at their beautiful home in the Free State, when the Press Gang and the team were royally entertained. His private rugby museum must be the envy of all South Africans!

A quiet but effective 'King of the Baggage' was Herman Visser, who did a difficult job efficiently and with charm. One did not hear him organising early in the morning and late at night, and one just had to pack the bags and leave them outside the hotel room, and then collect one's boarding pass at the airport. Believe me, it is a splendid way to travel, but occasionally certain 'characters' kept the Press Bus waiting!

Masseur to the team and private 'secretary' to manager Alun Thomas was Dave Goddess of Jo'burg, the 'Man in Red', who dashed on to the field looking like a 'professional' and played his part in keeping the show on the road. Peter Burke represented 'World Tours' Travel Agency and, like his company, was learning the job, with manager, John Holmes, making periodic visits to the side.

As for the South African hospitality and 'care for the press', I feel it was much better than was often appreciated, and the Press party was the largest ever to travel with an international rugby team and must present problems for the future. Obviously, it is good for the game that so many papers, both South African and British, were interested in the tour but one feels that the team, and the Press and media party, must be divided into two units for future overseas tours. In 1955 and 1959 there were only two British journalists covering the full tours but, by the end of the 1974 tour, there were 15 with three members of the BBC. There were seven South African journalists throughout the tour, many more appearing for the big matches, and four regular South

African photographers. It was a big party and the member Unions of the International Board will have to give the problem much thought. The Press Gang were amicable for most of the tour but one sensed that there were slight irritations on both sides towards the end, and much of this was due to the size of the party. Yet, at all times, the management, captain and players were most helpful to all members of the media.

The members of the British Press travelling for most of the tour were Vivian Jenkins (*Sunday Times*), Pat Marshall (*Daily Express*), Terry O'Connor (*Daily Mail*), John Reason (*Daily Telegraph*), David Frost (*Guardian*), Chris Lander (*Daily Mirror*), Ed van Esbeck (*Irish Times*), Colm Smith (*Irish Independent*) and myself. For the last three weeks there came John Reed (*Sunday Express*), Barry Newcombe (*Evening Standard*), Doug Ibbotson (*Evening News*), Bleddyn Williams (*People*), Clem Thomas (*Observer*) and Mike Austin (*Conventry Evening Telegraph*), and for the last week, Peter Batt (*Sun*). Forming the BBC party, which originated in Wales and not London, were Dewi Griffiths (TV Producer) Nigel Starmer-Smith (TV commentator) and Alun Williams (Sound commentator) while Terry O'Connor and myself did sound radio direct to London under the guidance of Sports Editor, Cliff Morgan.

Kim Shippey (English) and Gerhard Viviers (Afrikaans) were the SABC commentators throughout the tour while the South African pressmen with us, and many of them were old friends, included John du Toit, Quintus Van Rooyen, Neil Cameron, Herman le Roux, Mike Shafto, Hans Knoetze, Leon Gouws and the SAPA representative, David Raath. In addition there were four photographers John Rubython (Freelance, Cape Town), Gert Hattingh (Johannesburg), Eugene Labuschagne (Cape Town), and Wessel Oosthuizen (Johannesburg).

This was a big party and, of all these, I feel the prize for the 'hardest worker' should go to my good friend, Ed Van Esbeck, on his first tour and enjoying every minute of it, despite the fact that he was never without his typewriter and his phone. A fast talking, delightful Irishman, who should travel on many Lions tours in the future. As for Vivian and myself, following seven consecutive Lions tours together and millions of words, by cable, telephone, airmail and over the 'air', we are calling it a day from long tours. They are fun and full of interest but they are also hard work. Yet one would not have missed any of them and this last one least of all, although I cannot help feeling that the 'first' is always the best and happiest, a visit to 'wonderland', and so 1955 remains more in the memory than any of the others and whenever I chat to Cliff Morgan, Danny Davies, R. H. Williams, or any member of that favoured party, the year 1955 is mentioned. Perhaps, it is that 'Old Lions never die, they simply fade away!'

CHAPTER THREE

The Preamble

Every tour has to start somewhere and this one started on July 17, 1973 when the Four Home Rugby Unions announced the names of the Manager and his assistant, through the secretary of the Tours Committee, Albert Agar, a London banker. He told the press that Alun Thomas, a Swansea sales manager in a family business and 48-year-old former Welsh international and 1955 British Lion, would be the manager. A member of the WRU executive, a pioneer of coaching and squad training, and the assistant manager of the 1964 Welsh team in South Africa, and the first ever British coach to tour abroad. His assistant was the equally popular and experienced Syd Millar of Belfast, who had played 39 times for Ireland as a prop and made three Lions tours in 1959, 1962 and 1968, and who was in business in Northern Ireland.

Both were happy family men and much respected in British rugby, who knew South Africans and South African conditions extremely well. At the time of their selection they appeared an ideal pair, even though Vic Roberts (England), Handel Rogers (Wales) and Clive Rowlands (Wales) pushed them hard at the FHU interviews. The appointments were well received and immediately they were congratulated with offers of help from Manager Douglas Smith and Coach Carwyn James of the 1971 Lions side, and this cheered them. From the start, Thomas and Millar were in harmony whatever was to be their future in South Africa and they opened lines of communication which they and their wives will retain for many, many years.

They arranged to meet early and plan a winter campaign of observation of likely players and the preparation of plans for the tour. They needed a good team and thus the talent available had to be analysed in detail at club and international level and, more important, they had to get to know the people they wanted with them on tour. They knew, better than the selectors, what qualities made a good tourist since it was not always that the most brilliant player who made the best tourist. So they set about gathering all the knowledge possible from those who had gone before, in the cause of British rugby, to all corners of the globe. In rugby football no one man knows it all!

First, Thomas and Millar agreed about the captain. There was only one man, the 33-year-old William John McBride, a bank official from Belfast, the most capped rugby player in the world, who had four Lions tours behind him and a five-star performance as pack leader in New Zealand in 1971. He simply had to go to South Africa again and, as captain of Ireland, he was the one man the players would respect and follow. McBride had the qualities for he was a big man, a shrewd and generous man, a player with a purpose who thrived on responsibility. There would be nothing new for McBride on tour and despite the obvious challenges from John Pullin, Ian McLauchlan and Gareth Edwards, it simply had to be the 'Big Fella from Ballymena, who hated small men!' Thus the captain was selected far earlier than anyone realised and he was an unofficial member of the trio which virtually selected the side they wanted for the tour.

After this Alun Thomas and myself met many times and what we discussed must remain a secret, but many an item would have made headline news. We had remained friends since 1955 and the blood brotherhood of the Lions Club is something unique, as it was men like Rhys Gabe, Willie Llewellyn, Percy Bush, Tommy Vile, Stanger-Leathes, Charlie Patterson and Sammy Saunders, who introduced me to the 'mystique' of touring long before 1955, at their annual reunions of the 1904 side to Australia and New Zealand. One was fortunate to enjoy such an introduction and, in 1955, Vivian Jenkins, a worthy 1938 Lion, led me through Southern Africa in a tour that remains magical in the memory after 20 years. Even if I did pack his bag occasionally he more than repaid this small debt with his extensive knowledge and outrageous charm!

Alun Thomas was on the 1955 tour and Syd Millar on the 1959 tour and so I enjoyed a friendship that was forged in the cauldron of many famous test areas and over glasses of flowing wine in the early hours of the morning. Then there was something else that drew all together; the desire to become the first side to win a series in South Africa in this century. Yet there were battles ahead and not the least was the determination of a minority of the community to prevent the tour getting off the ground. We live in an age when minorities often rule, and the silent majority remain silent for the sake of peace. How long can such stupidity last?

The next major item for the consideration of the four Home Unions and the management was the itinerary, and this received very close scrutiny with Alun Thomas, working in harmony with the likeable and unobtrusive FHU honorary secretary, Albert Agar, the former England centre of the 1950's. Alun Thomas chatted to me about the fixtures list and Syd Millar and he had long conversations, attempting to formulate an ideal itinerary with a build up for each test in the area where it would be played.

Then Danie Craven flew in to London, privately, to meet the members of the FHU Tours Committee and the Management, asking that two stronger sides be met instead of the North West and North East Cape. This was a difficult point because South Africa wanted the Lions and the FHU held the ace card but, eventually, they gave way and agreed to play the Southern Universities at Cape Town and the Quaggas at Ellis Park. These were much harder matches and would provide far bigger gates, although each of the affected small district Unions would be compensated with handsome sums, far more than they would have taken in gate money at their respective matches.

It is true that the Lions beat the Universities 26–4 in pouring rain at Newlands before 20,000 spectators, but the Quaggas match nearly cost them their unbeaten record at 20–16 before 51,000 spectators in a midweek match. So the fixture list was the strongest possible and contained fewer easy matches than in the past, but there was full agreement when the itinerary was released in London and Cape Town on October 25, 1973.

The next item required by the management and approved by the FHU was a working-up centre in South Africa rather than a week at Eastbourne, which would not represent South African conditions. The FHU did not want any anti-apartheid demonstrations in the peaceful town of Eastbourne but the management's real desire was to work-up on the highveld near where the first match of the tour was being played at Potchefstroom. Management and press, on return from the 1962 tour, had suggested Stilfontein, near to Potchefstroom, as the ideal first base because it had a pleasant hotel in the Three Fountains, which could accommodate the side and camp followers, with training grounds adjacent. The town was small and quiet, and the weather ideal and the people friendly, and there would be no 'besieging' of the team before it had settled down. The SA Board agreed to the Lions leaving earlier, on May 6, and arriving in Stilfontein on May 7, with a first match at Potchefstroom against Western Transvaal on May 15. There would be 22 matches on tour including four tests at Cape Town, Pretoria, Port Elizabeth and Johannesburg, plus matches against the Coloureds and the Bantu.

With all this settled, the next and most important business was that of selecting the touring side. Alun Thomas and Syd Millar travelled thousands of miles in the four Home Countries during the 1973–74 season and watched every possible candidate before the Four Home Unions circulated over forty candidates asking them if they were available to travel. John Taylor was not considered as the only international player not prepared to travel, but three of those considered said they were not free to tour – David Duckham of England, Gerald Davies of Wales and Mike Gibson of Ireland, for personal and domestic reasons.

At the time, this was a blow as no one realised the Lions could win three and draw one test without these three players, highlighting the strength in depth of British rugby which did not reveal itself, easily, in the stalemate of the international championship. Although all three was interviewed and written to, by the management, they could not bring themselves to travel. However, before the team left, Davies and Gibson intimated that they would be available as replacements from the end of June.

As it turned out, Gibson was required to replace Old, and he travelled to play quite well in seven of the last ten matches, but he did not make the Third and Fourth Test, which must have proved a considerable disappointment to him, as Milliken and McGeechan held their places in the centre. Davies was sent for when Clive Rees was injured a second time and, after much persuasion, agreed to travel only to change his mind an hour later and tell the FHU it was not possible. Alan Morley travelled in his place and appeared in two matches out of a possible six. One cannot say what would have happened to the test XV had Davies arrived, as J. J. Williams was playing well and Irvine, the second place kicker, was doing nicely on the other wing.

It would have been embarrassing without anyone, selectors or players, being at fault. The absence of the three leading three-quarters at the start forced those selected to improve more rapidly and fill the gaps quite adequately. Milliken developed quickly and soundly; McGeechan was a reliable utility player; J. J. Williams, after a quiet start on heavy grounds, became a match winner and Irvine, as a fine full-back, moved up to become a test wing, in the manner of those two great former Springboks, Gerry Brand and Freddie Turner. Yet the back division set off with only two real world class players in Gareth Edwards and J. P. R. Williams, but the others advanced to meet the need, and the test series ended with the Lions scoring ten tries to one as against seven tries each in the New Zealand series of 1971.

One should remember this and not condemn the 1974 side, as some may well do, arguing that they did not use their backs. Ten tries in any four matches against the Springboks on their own ground is an achievement, with only one against, in the second half of the fourth match. Again, J. J. Williams, whom Carwyn James said would do well on hard grounds, fulfilled the promise after leaving the mud of Cape Town and got two super tries in each of the Second and Third Tests, all as the result of good back play and individual flair.

While preparations went ahead in South Africa with the staging of the tour, the international matches at home found players bidding for places. The travel and accommodation organisation went to a new company, 'World Tours' of Cape Town, whom it is reported was backed by the SA Board with a financial interest and by former Springbok, the new tycoon, Jan Pickard. Unfortunately, this organisation, through a lack of experience, could not compare with South African Railways, who had looked after us in the past, and their young representative, Peter Burke, son of the 1970 All Blacks manager, though pleasant enough, could not match the 'know how' of the 'veteran' travelman, Bruce Hay of Cape Town. However hard 'World Tours' tried, one does feel that a Lions tour, at this stage of their company's development, was rather too much for them, and FHU may well ask for something different for the next Lions tour in SA, whenever it may be.

In January 1974, the Lions selectors, one from each of the FHU in Sandy Sanders (England), Clive Rowlands (Wales), Lex Govan (Scotland) and Fraser McMullen (Ireland), together with Thomas and Millar started in earnest to sort the 'wheat from the chaff' as the press in all four countries put forward their ideas and suggestions. The *Western Mail* said, 'Four in line for the captaincy, McBride, Pullin, Edwards and McLauchlan.' The *Daily Telegraph* said, 'McLauchlan has ideal credentials to lead Lions.' *The Times* said, 'Gibson's withdrawal is blow to Lions,' followed by, Lions' tour coming apart at seams.' The *Sunday Times,* never in favour of the tour, unfortunately, said, 'Rugby Crisis: Lions lose their roar.' Finally, before the selection, the *Western Mail* forecast that McBride would be captain and Wales could have ten players in the party. They had nine, with Derek Quinnell missing out, as he was not 100 per cent fit at the time but, by the end of the season, was the outstanding forward in the WRU Cup Final. He was one of the genuinely unlucky ones.

There were other unlucky players including Peter Dixon of England, Terry Cobner (Wales), and Alaistair McHarg (Scotland), while his omission came as a shock to John Pullin, the England captain. When the team was announced in South Africa, the chairman of selectors, Johaan Classen remarked, 'This unknown Bobby Windsor must be good to get in ahead of Pullin.' A prophetic comment as Windsor hooked in all four tests! Dr Danie Craven made a bold prophecy, 'This could be the best side ever to tour South Africa. An excellent squad!' Ken Kennedy, at 31 years of age, was recalled after a lapse of eight years (1966 Lions) as the other hooker and proved an invaluable choice. Not only was he a good tourist, played well and helped morale, but was outstanding and devoted as medical adviser to the side and the press gang.

Generally, the team was well received by followers of the game, although one critic did not hide his disappointment that McBride was honoured with the captaincy, believing that he was too old to ensure a test place, while many critics pointed out the weakness at three-quarter and lack of experience on the wings but agreed that the forwards, overall, were a likely lot. The main barrage of criticism that hit the headlines of the British press, following the announcement of the side, was political.

The Labour Government advised the FHU, through its Minister

of Sport, Mr Denis Howell, to 'call off the tour'. He asked for an early meeting with the FHU to 'advise them of the strong feelings we have about this tour.' Immediately, Albert Agar replied, 'We are determined to go to South Africa. It won't make any difference what Mr Howell says, but if he wants to see us we are quite willing.' The meeting was held and Mr John Tallent, chairman of the FHU, accompanied Mr Agar. The Government did not ban the tour, much as they would have liked to have done, while Mr Howell was man enough to go to London Airport to congratulate the Lions on their return.

John Tallent, who has become a rugby ambassador at large during the past 10 years, was at Cape Town to see the Lions win the First Test, and Albert Agar was at Port Elizabeth and Johannesburg to watch the last two and return home on the Sunday to help Tallent arrange a champagne reception for the Lions at Heathrow Airport on the Tuesday morning. All's well that ends well, and the FHU were completely vindicated, but for several players it was a sacrifice. Yet the determination and fine play on the field and behaviour off it, plus the new glory achieved for British sport, won the support of many previously uncommitted and even caused Peter Hain to do a 'volta face'!

There were several people outside rugby football who did not wish the Lions to tour, a few for genuine moral reasons but, in the main, for political reasons and the 'bandwaggoners' were out shouting from the hilltops. From the Prime Minister and his Cabinet down to the local councillors and many churchman who had never seen the Southern Cross, they shouted 'outrageous' and 'stop them', while most of them enjoyed food or goods each day imported from South Africa. Every man holding a British passport was entitled to visit South Africa. Britain was still a free country, and thus each citizen was entitled to make a free choice. Peter Hain left South Africa to use Britain as a base to attack his 'beloved country'. Why then should he deny a Briton the right to visit South Africa and see for himself?

Like Alun Thomas, I do not support apartheid, and realise there must be an easing of the situation in South Africa, but it is not as tense as many would have us believe. Certainly, not some sections of the British Press, yet I admire the *Guardian* for sending its rugby writer, David Frost, to cover the tour although strongly opposed to the South African Government. The *Sunday*

Times is anti-apartheid in its sports pages but its rugby writer was there to report on the rugby played, in his traditional dignified and accurate manner. Indeed, the *Mirror* had its man there and, unfortunately, he was to have done it for the *Times,* but his by-line appeared in both papers simultaneously, and this brought an abrupt end to the contract!

The two leading Eire dailies, the *Irish Times* and the *Irish Independent,* sent their rugby writers who provided extensive coverage as did most of those papers who did send someone, with the *Sun* rushing out one of its soccer writers to cover the last week of the tour, as readers had complained about the coverage. Pat Marshall fed the Express Group faithfully before the final three weeks of the tour brought colleagues John Reed (*Sunday Express*) and Barry Newcombe (*Evening Standard*), together with Doug Ibbotson (*Evening News*) and Mike Auston (*Coventry Evening Chronicle*), to the scene of activity. At least Rugby Football had captured the imagination of the 'soccer' papers, and a good thing too, for the papers and the game, while the FHU had been completely vindicated in their decision, as politicians jockeyed for position to meet the Lions at Heathrow on July 30 and smile for the cameras. What a pity Miss Joan Lestor could not bring herself to attend the homecoming, as she would have found that the 1974 Lions did not bite or offend, and were truly loyal to the country she helped to govern.

Towards the end of March my own paper published a leader in which it said, 'The British Lions tour of South Africa should go ahead. This is not said with any degree of enthusiasm, for the *Western Mail* has no wish to encourage the South African African Government and its suicidal apartheid policy. We believe that it should take place because such a ban, unaccompanied by similar sanctions on all contacts, sporting, cultural and social, and one imposed by the international community, would be unrealistic and of doubtful value... Contacts with South Africa, however limited and artificial they may be, can do no harm. They are valuable in that they bring to us some knowledge of that country and give to it some information about us and our views of apartheid.'

I was glad to see my paper declare its hand for, as Sports Editor, I had never once been instructed to write for or against the tour, and was given a completely free hand. This was 'freedom of the press' at its best, and I respected it by rarely, if ever, introducing politics into the sports pages. In the News sections and Readers' Letters section of the paper however, both points of view were freely expressed. Welsh rugby wanted the tour to take place, although few, if any, favoured apartheid, but the clubs and their officials, as always, divorced their politics from their sport and supported the tour. They had no 'double standards' and my admiration for Welsh rugby remains intense, as when the tour was over Welshmen, of all beliefs, welcomed back the returning heroes, some of whom had toured without pay.

At the end of the tour, the *Rand Daily Mail*, which is an anti-South African Government paper, published a leader which contained the following, 'The British Lions came to South Africa nearly three months ago because of their love for rugby and their desire to prove themselves the world's leaders by beating the Springboks. There was, of course, also another dimension. After the opposition to their tour at home, their coming here was an act of courage; more, the thought of playing with apartheid must have been a source of worry to at least some of them. The Lions have explained that they believed they could make a greater contribution towards non-racialism in sport – and thus, South Africa's eventual re-entry into full international competition – by coming rather than staying away ... we hope the Lions will return; we hope too that Springbok team will again soon play them on their home ground. It's up to South Africa to make it happen.'

I believe they will, even it if takes a little more time then the impatient world demands. Dr Koornhof, the new Minister of Sport, educated as a Rhodes Scholar at Oxford University, is a broadminded, enlightened member of the South African Government and he will proceed at the fastest possible rate allowed by the extreme right of his party. He wants merit trials, and the next two years will be all important since one saw very definite signs of advancement. However, one must remember, too, that coloured or native players, Proteas or Leopards, must be worthy of their places before they are chosen.

The coloureds are split into two groups, with the larger group being non-cooperative with the other coloured section, known as the Proteas, with the Africans known as the Leopards. So all is not easy, but if coloured or native players are included in a national South African side after merit trials then it would open wide the doors for South Africa's re-entry into the rugby world. The International Board, whose members visited South Africa after its Sydney conference, will not close the doors, but will leave them open for the South African Rugby Board to continue their fight to obtain permission for merit trials. These almost came about last year but there was a last minute hitch, even before the Lions arrived. Again, the Quaggas were on the brink of receiving permission to include two coloured players against the Lions, and this would have been a major step forward but, unfortunately, a journalist trying to be far too clever, broke the story in Johannesburg, before the Government could say 'yes'. If only that writer had held his pen for forty-eight hours it would have happened and the Quaggas were bitterly disappointed.

I feel the Lions tour did much more good for the cause of multi-racial sport than anyone at home can imagine. They revealed skill and dignity. They got to know coloureds and Africans as much as they did people of European descent. They played against all races. They proved ambassadors and, in Alun Thomas, they had the perfect diplomat as manager and when the great day comes, he will have done much in the last twenty years to have helped it because he is interested in all the people of South Africa. He is a sportsman and not a politician. The 1974 Lions were all sportsmen and if, occasionally, travelling pressmen expressed different views, they were never those of the majority of the party. In the six years since I travelled with the 1968 team much has happened and much more will happen. The people in the British Isles, shouting to break off contact, are missing the boat. You cannot have your penny and the bun. Allow sport to come to terms with itself, and the sportsmen of other countries to meet each other regularly.

For South Africa as a whole general progress is being made, but it will have to be slow as the coloured and native populations are passing through stages in their evolution that are quite different from those of the European. The need is for increased pay; better education; improved technical training; medical attention and housing, and there have been considerable strides since 1968. There will be more, and soon one can hope for selected franchise and a quicker development of the 'homelands' or bantustans. There is much to be done, but it will not happen overnight and, as one rich Indian in Natal told me, 'We do not want another Nigeria or Uganda, and European politicians know little of the problems that exist here.' I recall now the remark of Vivian Jenkins to Basil Kenyon, as we met the happy people of Transkei, 'If only the British Government would come here and see what we have seen today!'

As Dr Danie Craven, a true liberal, wrote for the ***Western Mail*** before the tour, 'South Africa is a controversial country; we are in the news; we have become a focal point in world events; we are criticised and we are condemned in many places, but we will not try to influence anybody into liking us. Everybody visiting South Africa is his or her own judge of what we are, and whether we are liked or not we can still respect and admire those self same people who did not like us. I am saying this so that the Lions may know that as far as we are concerned they will be welcome, irrespective of what their feelings during the tour may be.'

The Lions were welcomed everywhere and applauded readily as they left the field at Port Elizabeth, where they clinched the test series for the first time this century. They were welcomed at almost every airport by thousands of people of all races, and never more so than at East London before the match against the Leopards. Everyone praised them for coming and only a few, very few, criticised them. Their off the field behaviour was the best of any touring team and if some papers magnified certain small incidents, they were doing it purely in the cause of 'circulation' and not in the interest of rugby football or good relationships between the two countries.

Hotel managers spoke highly of them. Liaison officers loved them. Schoolboys adored them for they never refused to sign autographs or talk to them at any time. The work that was done beforehand; the determination to do well and to lift the image of British sport, the desire to live as a happy unit, the general good sense of humour, and the respect for the noblest Lion of them all, Willie John McBride, made this the most successful and the greatest of Lions tours.

CHAPTER FOUR

The First Scrum

The first experience of flying in a Jumbo Jet is quite remarkable even for someone who has flown many thousands of miles in the two hemispheres, and the very size of this remarkable heavier-than-air machine sees the childhood memories of Jules Verne fade from the scene. It appeared as broad in the beam as my old destroyer and possibly longer. It was comfortable with more room for the legs and bags than the 707, and if Boeing need a press agent in the United Kingdom then I would offer my services since there can be no difficulty in getting people to 'fly jumbo'. I was on a South African Airways flight and enjoyed the service, while watching an up to date Elizabeth Taylor film *Nightwatch* into the early morning was, even for a hardened traveller, a refreshing experience. She is still a beautiful woman and I am sorry that the 'Welshman' who is so keen on rugby, is parted from her.

Never having been able to sleep on aircraft, I found the 13½ hour journey a long one, as the Lions had found it so a week earlier, but believed it was a good idea to get the flight over and done with in one hop since, as Willie John McBride pointed out, 'You can only see the clouds up there and the occasional sunset and sunrise.' It was chilly in the early morning at Jan Smuts Airport but Joshua and his Mercedes drove me carefully to Potchefstroom along the almost straight, flat road out of Johannesburg through the Western Transvaal. The clouds sailed high across the blue sky like galleons, their bases clear cut and one felt they were just 'passing' with no intent to wet the dry earth beneath them. In this part of the world they get more rain in the summer than winter and I was told that the summer 'had been good' with rain for crops following two bad dry summers. Later farmer/rugby writer John Du Toit was to confirm this. Potchefstroom was the scene of the first match but the team were at the Three Fountains Hotel at Stilfontein, some 30 kilometres to the west, a clean, healthy, attractive new mining town, not yet 30 years of age. It looked as it did in 1962, and my first Lions contact was Willie John McBride, who looked so slim, hard and fit in the morning sun after training, that one could not but be impressed. At that moment he looked a leader.

Then to Alun Thomas, who greeted me as did Livingstone the searching Stanley, although it was but two weeks since we had last met. The first seven days had been hectic for him with nearly 40 South African pressmen and women seeking him out for interviews; many official and social functions and the setting up of an organisation at the hotel with the big, happy Syd Millar. All would have been well but for the tragic lack of courtesy on the part of the British Foreign Office and I was deeply surprised that Foreign Minister Jim Callaghan, a rugby follower and a Cardiff MP, could allow a lesser assistant minister to issue such a statement that said the British Government, in as many words, was turning its back on the Lions teams.

It hurt Manager Thomas very much indeed, for deep down in his heart, he is a kind, sensitive Welshman, and he was the first sporting manager in the history of British teams abroad to be virtually 'disowned' by his government. Can you think the government of any other country in the world would have acted so spitefully? Alun Thomas did not comment at first but a private conversation with officials and trusted pressmen was overheard by a cub reporter and the obvious and justifiable comment made privately by Thomas, that it was a 'stab in the back', was cabled round the world from Jo'burg.

Always a diplomat in public, Thomas was distressed by this intrusion of privacy and for a couple of days he worried about future relationships with the South African press but was quickly assured that the official tour party would respect his confidence and never quote him on such matters, which are delicate at all times, without formal permission. This is standard procedure and as we chatted he felt happy that at least we could chat over the more difficult points arising from press matters in a friendly way and share our problems. The team were most friendly in their greeting and there were some members of the party I had not chatted to, individually, before and they made me welcome in a manner that suggested they would prove good tourists, because first impressions are important. Tom David confessed, 'I have never trained as hard as we have been doing here at Stilfontein, either for Llanelli or Wales!' It was happy news for my ears and I knew that Syd Millar had been man enough to accept the advice of Carwyn James who, also, almost 'killed' his charges in the opening weeks. For Millar it was more difficult, since he had the change of altitude to contend with, but the itinerary had been well planned and the start on the highveld was all important.

The first day in South Africa soon passed for me and I was ready for Match Number One the next day, May 15, to start yet another Lions tour in the bright sunshine of the Southern Hemisphere. Syd Millar was frank, 'I want a win for the side, and even a three points margin will do, but I hope we score many more. We are going to run at the opposition with the ball and play good football. I want that on this tour because I believe the lads are capable of good stuff.' In this first match his wish was to be granted for the 1974 Lions started where the 1971 Lions had ended!

Match No. 1 at Olen Park, Potchefstroom. May 15, 1974.
British Isles defeated Western Transvaal by seven goals, three penalties and two tries (59) to one goal, one penalty and one try (13).
Crowd: 25,000. *Weather:* Dry and sunny. *Ground:* Hard with grass covering.
Scorers:
British Isles – G. Brown, W. Steele, J. Maloney, A. Ripley, T. David(2), G. Edwards(2) and C. Rees tries; P. Bennett seven cons and three pens.
Western Transvaal – J. Stoffberg and I. Schaap tries. W. de Bruin one con. one pen.
Teams:
WESTERN TRANSVAAL: W. de Bruin; I. Schaap, P. Roodt, T. Van der Berg, J. Van der Merwe; C. Taylor, M. Benade; S. Raath, P. de Wet, J. Burger, J. Tromp, P. Brand, T. Jacobs, J. Stoflberg and R. Owen (capt.).
BRITISH ISLES: J. P. R. Williams; W. C. C. Steel R. T. E. Bergiers, I. R. McGeechan, C. Rees; P. Bennett, J. J. Maloney; J. McLauchlan, R. W. Windsor, A. B. Carmichael, W. J. McBride, G. L. Brown, T. P. David, A. G. Ripley and A. Neary.
Replacements: G. O. Edwards for Maloney (4 mins second

half); F. E. Cotton for Carmichael (30 mins second half)
Referee: Mr Piet Robbertse (Eastern Transvaal).

The Lions received a standing ovation from the crowd on making their way from their coach to the dressing room and this must have warmed their hearts, considering that they had been much criticised outside the rugby world for making the visit. When they took the field with McBride holding the 'Lion' high, there was another roar and the sight of the scarlet jerseys once again, plus the giant figure of the captain, quickened the pulse a little. The tour was on at last, and the 12 months of preparation was about to be put to the test. However much one does off the field, it is the 80 minutes of actual play that is all important for the record book. There is much more to a long tour than the rugby but in 20 years time it will be the match results that are read and discussed by the rugby 'faithful' of both countries.

Five minutes from the start the giant Scottish lock, Gordon Brown, had crashed over for the first try of the tour and he said afterwards, 'I was so happy at this I felt the tears coming to my eyes. It was a big thrill!' The movement had been started as the result of a superb crash tackle by Bergiers during a Western Transvaal attack and he combined with Neary to set David running like a bullock. The crowd roared at this because they love forward charges in South Africa, and David sent Brown over for a try that Bennett failed to convert, but this was only one of two failures in a dozen kicks at goal during the afternoon.

Next came a penalty goal from Bennett when a scrum collapsed and his kick slipped gently over the cross bar from fifty yards. Bergiers again crash tackled and gathered to send Steele away for a fine try under the posts. Bennett converted and the Lions had 13 points on the board in 10 minutes. Great stuff, and in the back of one's mind as one typed and tabulated, there were distant visions of 1971. It was the pace and support work of the forwards and the accuracy of the handling that impressed as the Lions, under Millar's instructions, ran at the opposition. Again, the feed back was good from the mauls and Maloney and Bennett worked smoothly at half-back.

Then followed a spirited challenge from Western Transvaal. They collected a forty yard penalty from de Bruin, a high kicking full-back, before Maloney scored a delightful elusive try and Bennett converted. Then prop Raath charged through the short line in the Lions '25' to dash on and pass inside to No. 8 Stoffberg, who scored an unconverted try. This movement had started under the old line-out law and one sensed that the South Africans had given up the enforcement of the new law. The Westerns got another try, a good one, when Bennett had a clearing kick charged down on the right and the opposition moved left for wing Schaap to kick on and regather to score and de Bruin to kick a good goal. Back came the Lions with an easy penalty from Bennett after obstruction and at half time it was 22–13, and the tour had been blessed with an excellent start. The heavy Westerns pack, averaging over 16 st. per man, had gone well to test the Lions but it was the thrusting pace of the tourists that impressed and the graceful round the corner accuracy of Bennett as a place kicker while he was ready for a sudden probing dart in attack; a feature that was encouraging for all.

At the interval, two young ladies took to the field in yellow hot pants with a tray of orange slices for each team, and this was sight to raise the blood pressure of any Home Unions representative. 'Wow,' said the British pressmen, 'Fancy this at Twickers!' Even at my advanced age, I thought it an innovation of charm if lacking in tradition.

The second half began with a steal-away try from the back of the scrum by Andy Ripley, rightly christened 'Geronimo', which Bennett converted and from then on it was a one-sided match. The Western Transvaal forwards just could not carry their weight round the field at the pace demanded of them by the Lions, while the tourists improved in every phase. Maloney left the field injured early in the second half with a dislocated collar bone and Gareth Edwards entered the scene like a Lion ready to feed after the 'kill' had been made. He helped himself to two tries, one a superb slicing effort from a short penalty, and the back row dominated while the three-quarters ran delightfully, as the halves sent them away.

McGeechan looked good and Rees full of pace. McBride was superb in the line-out peel-off and Bennett kicked in the manner of Barry John. The end came at 59–13 and few could not have been satisfied with this performance. Having finished my *Western Mail* report I chatted away to the BBC with first Gareth Edwards,

Right: The 2nd test at Pretoria. Gareth Edwards gets his kick in, challenged by Morne du Plessis (*Rod Samson, Rand Daily Mail*).

Middle: The 2nd test. A determined Fergus Slattery bursts away from a loose maul, with the entire Springbok pack in pursuit! (*Jan Nel, Rand Daily Mail*).

Below: Willie John McBride leaps high in the line-out (*The Argus*).

Above left: Andy Irvine, the Lions' top point scorer (*Basil Hall, Eastern Province Herald*).

Above right: J. P. R. Williams makes a magnificent clearance (*Allen Lipschitz*).

Below: Andy Ripley sports a special tee shirt (*Gert Hattingh, Die Transvaler*).

always good value, and then former Scottish international, Chick Henderson, who drowned 'Old Man River' in 1968, about the day's play. Edwards was optimistic about the tour and Henderson thought it would be a great series while I forecast bravely that McBride would emerge as the star of the tour. The evening was pleasant and many old friends were met at the reception including Johaan Classen, Wilf Rosenberg and Corrie Borneman, proving that rugby holds many friendships for all who participate in any grade. The S. A. Minister of Sport spoke and greeted the Lions while praising them for coming. Alun Thomas started his long series of after-match speeches and uttered a few words in Afrikaans. Brave fellow, but the early hours of the morning at the hotel found the echo of rugby songs through the corridors. The tour was on the road!

The flight from Jan Smuts Airport was a pleasant one with excellent food and drink supplied by SAA and this helped to pass the journey rapidly, but one regretted that little could be seen of the famous Kalahari Desert. Sitting in Jan Smuts Airport brought back memories of the sad farewells of several Lions sides as they set off for home without having trapped the Springboks. I recall one amazing party there in 1968 when Manager Brooks and his 'high flyers' said goodbye in champagne. I believe officials were slightly relieved to see them go but they were never as bad as some writers suggested, and they did enjoy themselves.

Windhoek is the capital of South West Africa, with a population of 65,000, of which 36,000 are whites, 5,000 coloured, some of whom are attractive and delicately figured with hips that would have matched Betty Grable, and 24,000 Bantu. Of the white population, sixty per cent speak Afrikaans, thirty-four per cent German and six per cent English, although this figure was marginally increased during the stay of the Lions at the Continental Hotel where the charming German manageress and her staff poured thick steaks and lager beer into the mouths of their British guests. Amazingly clean, an oasis in the desert, it is an excellent place for purchasing presents for wives and sweethearts and the Windhoek lager beer is really good. One missed the portly figure of film star Gert Frober leading a German Brass Band and a little high stepping.

The city is the home of one, Jan Ellis, a leading Springbok

flanker, said to train six days a week running over the local hills. A frightening thought for the average British rugby player, but Ellis is a fine test performer and when he led his men on to the sun-drenched rugby stadium before a capacity crowd of 12,000 home supporters basking in their shirts sleeves and coloured frocks, he had already played in 31 tests for South Africa and, at 31 years of age, was eager to prove that he was still the best flanker in the land. Two selectors, including the pleasant chairman of the panel, Johan Classen, were in the stand to watch this player, known rather as a 'loner' in the South West and a quiet fellow, but certainly the darling of the crowd which gave him a special cheer as he headed his determined team on to the field.

Match No. 2 at Rugby Stadium, Windhoek. May 18, 1974.
British Isles defeated South West Africa by one goal, three penalties and two tries (23) to one goal two penalties and one try (16).
Crowd: 12,000. *Weather:* Sunny with breeze. *Ground:* Very hard with grass cover.
Scorers:
British Isles – G. O. Edwards, C. Rees and R. Milliken tries. A. Old one pen. A. Irvine one con. and two pens.
South West Africa – J. Ellis and W. Prinsloo tries. D. Karg one con. two pens.
Teams:
SOUTH WEST AFRICA: J. Smuts; N. Smith, B. Meyer, K. Gerishuys, W. Prinsloo; D. Karg, T. Van Zyl; B. de Jongh, P. Van der Nerwe, H. Coetzee, J. Coetzee, T. Van Rensburg, J. Ellis (capt.), H. Schrader, and G. Parker.
BRITISH ISLES: A. R. Irvine; C. Rees, G. W. Evans, R. A. Milliken, J. J. Williams; A. G. B. Old, G. O. Edwards (capt.); J. McLauchlan, K. W. Kennedy, F. E. Cotton, C. W. Ralston, R. M. Uttley, T. David, T. M. Davies, J. F. Slattery.
Referee: Mr C. de Bruyn (Transvaal).

From the kick off the South West played as if their very lives depended upon the result of the match, and they pressurised the Lions continually before taking the lead after four minutes with an easy 15 yard penalty by outside-half Deon Karg, when the Lion's midfield players were trapped offside at a ruck. After ten minutes Old landed a penalty goal in his second attempt, from 15 yards, when the South West were penalised at a ruck.

Yet this did not herald a breakthrough by the Lions as they appeared much less forceful than at Potchefstroom, and said later that there were moments when they felt their lungs would burst in the heat and the altitude of the highest representative rugby ground in the world.

Yet the real trouble was the pace, vigour and determination of the South West team, playing above themselves and delighting their supporters. Then came two typical tries from the two great rival captains, Gareth Edwards and Jan Ellis. First, the one by Edwards when Davies picked up from the back of a scrum five and fed his captain moving to the blind side. Edwards charged through one tackle and was half held by another, but the ball did not touch the ground and he squeezed over in the corner. Old could not kick the goal and five minutes later from a scrum five outside the Lions line, Ellis picked up and crashed over on the open side. Karg kicked an easy goal and the (jubilant) South West were in the lead at 9–7.

Five minutes from the end of the first half, number eight Schrader punched Alan Old in the face after a tackle and Andy Irvine, experiencing an unhappy first half against the high kicks directed at him, was called up to take the kick and he landed a good penalty goal from 30 yards. At the interval is was 10–9 to the Lions but far from comfortable. Sitting in the very back row of the high stand in the heat of the late afternoon one's mind raced back to Brisbane in 1971 when the Lions lost their first match of that tour and Manager Doug Smith gave the actual cause of defeat as 'disrhythmia'!

What could Manager Alun Thomas say this time if the day was lost? Could it be the heat, the altitude, the rarefied atmosphere that found the heart pounding and the lungs bursting or the forceful play of the South West? The Lions forwards were slow to the breakdown and although enjoying superiority at the line-out, won little crisp ball for Edwards and he was back on his heels, doing his defensive, covering and clearing act once again, as he had done for Wales in the previous season. The Lions, having played with the sun and breeze, turned to face it and opponents thirsting for their first every victory over an official touring side.

If the first half was worrying, the second proved even worse for Lions in the stand and their camp followers. However, they got a second try when the backs moved smartly from a line-out and Milliken kicked cleverly for Rees to run on to the ball and gather before dashing over for a good try as he was tackled, but Irvine was just wide with his conversion attempt. Back came the South West with the most spectacular try of the match when left-wing Willelm Prinsloo, in his thirties, dashed inside between his two centres, took the pass and cut the Lions line to race on and beat Irvine at the corner for the try which Karg could not convert. At 13–14 the South West worked really hard for 15 minutes before Slattery was caught offside standing back from a maul, which was still on the line of touch, and so Karg kicked a 27 yard penalty to make it 16–14; put his side in sight of victory and raise the blood pressure of the crowd! Five minutes of facing the threat of disaster was as much as the Lions, on and off the field, could stand and they got down to the South West '25' where they launched a well-rehearsed attack that produced the winning score and brought much relief to themselves.

At a line-out, Davies tapped down and Cotton took it well to peel and commit before handing on to Edwards who set his line moving and (it was) Milliken who raced over for Irvine to kick a fine goal, making it 20–16. Healthier, of course, but still not safe. and when the South West were penalised at a set scrum, Irvine recovered most of his lost marks by kicking a 30 yard goal and it was 23-16 at the end. The Lions had not played well but had won, which was the important thing. The match ended with two typical Edwards' acts of defiance; a long raking 70 yard touch line kick from his own '25' and then a touch line charge that knocked over four South West forwards. It was enough to suggest that the Lions just deserved their win but one had to tell readers and listeners at home that the South West had played remarkably well.

The Civic reception was most pleasant and it was enjoyable to discuss rugby with Johaan Classen. I remember saying to him that the Lions had become of age in their approach, and that in recent years they played an 'adult' game with a much different, yet still attractive, approach. The wine flowed and the songs were sung but not quite as loudly, I thought, as at Stilfontein. The moment of truth had arrived . . . after all . . . it was hard to win in South Africa!

On Sunday we flew out of Windhoek for the Cape, the fairest Cape in all the world, little knowing that my story for the Echo, cabled in the afternoon had not reached Thomson House Cardiff until midnight on Saturday, this fact, when appreciated on Monday, was to shake my faith in what had been, hitherto, an excellent operation in communication. Now even that was breaking down and one felt a little remote and sad because cabling from New Zealand has been so easy with the time lag. Obviously, the South African and British combined service had gone adrift somewhere. A most worrying affair because one simply pours copy into the teleprinters at the grounds where matches are being played, at considerable expense, and just hope that they will reach the other end in time. The modern world can put men on the moon but the normal communication of fifty years ago is now well below par and this took the edge off the tour, at least for the British Press and their Editors, at this stage! My sympathies went out to Vernon Wigmore of the Echo, wanting to put his evening paper on the street with up-to-date Lions news.

There was a large and warm welcome waiting for the Lions at Capetown Airport with thousands out on Sunday afternoon to cheer them in, the tourists appreciated it for there is nothing like being made to feel at home when 7,000 miles away. The newcomers in the party were deeply impressed by the scenery of the Cape and the truly superb Table Mountain. Once again, it was the famous Arthur's Seat Hotel at Seapoint and it holds many happy memories for me, while Sylvia and Vivian Duggan did me proud with an evening meal at the Kelvin Club near Newlands, and in the discussion with them and their friends about the future of South Africa, one did not find them speaking with admiration about Mr Wilson or Miss Joan Lestor. The point made was this . . . 'The British Empire no longer exists and why are these people putting their noses into our affairs and how much does Miss Lestor really know about Africa, and particularly South Africa?' Mr Duggan, very much a liberal, who was in the RAF during the War and Cardiff-born complained, 'We try to project the image of Britain as the last great democracy, but this government embarrasses all of us who are liberal minded. Thank goodness the Lions have come, and South Africans can meet real British and Irish people.'

Former Springbok centre of the 1930s, Dr Louis Babrow

and his family had the same viewpoint but did say that things could improve and that the Four Home Unions must work hard on the South African Rugby Board to get mixed trials. Thus a lot of sensible people in South Africa are moving in the right direction, but Britain could no longer beat the drum from afar with high idealism while desperately needing to trade with South Africa. There can be no double standard.

The weather was just perfect on this first visit to the Cape with the sun shining down and a holiday atmosphere prevailing It was enough to send me to the beach for half an hour to test the waters of the Atlantic Ocean. The sand there was not as good as that of Rhossilli Bay and there was far too much seaweed but the water, the sun, and the pretty ladies were some compensation for the long distance traveller. The next match was at Wellington, in the wine growing district of the Boland, and as we drove there in the press bus I was surprised to hear from SABC commentator, Kim Shippey, a most helpful companion on tour, that South Africa now exports much of its best wine to Canada and Japan, and there were some good 'reds' missing from the lists. Gordon Bagnall, a local expert, later told me all about it.

Match No. 3 at Wellington. May 22, 1974.
British Isles defeated Boland by two goals three penalties and three tries (33) to two penalties (6).
Crowd: 21,500. *Weather:* Sunny and very hot. *Ground:* Hard with grass.
Scorers:
British Isles – T. O. Grace, W. J. McBride, G. O. Edwards and R. A. Milliken(2) A. G. B. Old two cons and three pens.
Boland – D. Visser and J. Theart pens.
Teams:
BOLAND: D. Visser; I. Van der Merwe, V. Odenaal, D. Mostert, R. La Roux; J. Theart, B. Wolmarans; N. Rossoun, H. Reyneke, D. Van der Merwe, J. Du Toit (capt), M. Craven, U. de Jager, D. Schreuder, D. du Plessis.
BRITISH ISLES: J. P. R. Williams; T. O. Grace, R. A. Milliken, I. R. McGeechan, J. J. Williams; A. G. B. Old, G. O. Edwards; F. E. Cotton, R. W. Windsor, A. B. Carmichael, W. J. McBride (capt), G L. Brown, T. P. David, A. G. Ripley, A. Neary.
Referee: Mr G. Bezuidenhout (Transvaal).

It was really hot when the Lions arrived in Wellington and a capacity crowd merely added to the warmth. No programmes could be purchased but there was fresh hope that the cables would get through more quickly as the Post Office operators had linked up with London Telex direct. The curtain raisers had to be watched and one was reasonably exhausted by the time they ended and the Lions took the field to a good welcome; to suggest it was a warm welcome would be the understatement of the tour. From the kick off the much fancied Boland attacked with a high kick but it was the Lions who took the lead with a penalty by Old from 43 yards following offside play in the loose after seven minutes. Then followed hard but unspectacular play as the Lions forwards battled for control. Visser kicked just wide with a 50 yard penalty attempt for Boland and Edwards later marked and dropped for goal before Milliken, Brown and Edwards were almost over in quick succession.

Obviously, the Lions having set out to control and not mess about, achieved their objective and, when Tom Grace got his first try of the tour following an Edwards and David move to the blind side, any prospect of defeat disappeared. Old kicked another penalty after 30 minutes from 28 yards for offside play in the loose and the Lions led by ten points at the interval despite the intense heat.

As he admitted afterwards, Willie John McBride found the effects of the heat more intense in the early stages of the second half... 'I suppose it was the interval break that did it for had we played non-stop I doubt whether it would have been so hard, but we got our second wind and the boys went well.' There didn't appear to be so much trouble with the interpretation of the laws although McBride did speak to Mr Bezuidehout, occasionally, and this was mainly about offside play at the rucks and mauls. Then came Old's third penalty, this time from 12 yards after a ruck where a Boland forward was offside as the Lions won the ball and went away, but the referee waited for the advantage law to operate before awarding the penalty. Then came the second try when Old punted high to the left corner where La Roux failed to gather and John J. Williams was up to collect and send Dick Milliken over for a try that Old converted.

The England outside-half appeared much happier and enjoyed

his afternoon of kicking, while showing much better judgement than at Windhoek, and Gareth Edwards was a constant menace to the Boland defence as a runner and kicker. Full-back Visser kicked a 40 yard penalty for Boland before Milliken got his second try when first the ball was moved out to Grace on the right and then back inside for the centre to gather and dodge over but Old could not convert. At this stage Tom David pulled a hamstring and was forced to leave the field and be replaced by Roger Uttley. Before the next score, a penalty for Boland by outside-half Theart, there was a short punch up between the front rows. It subsided quickly and then Gordon Brown gathered a high clearing kick 40 yards out and set off for the line with McBride in support, and when Brown was tackled he slipped to McBride who crashed over for a try that any locks would have been proud to have achieved late in a match.

Old kicked a superb goal and then, as the crowd started to leave the field, Edwards put the finishing touches to a fine afternoon's performance by the Lions, with a superb blindside dash from a ruck that brought him his fourth try of the tour that was not converted. The match ended at 33 points to 6 and it was convincing enough to restore the shaken confidence of the Lions following the torture of Windhoek. The forwards had played so much better and their drive had returned while Edwards was again in form and Old was so much happier while John Williams at full-back was steady and strong. Yet it was hot; the hottest day for any match I have watched overseas, even hotter than the France/Wales match in Paris in 1959.

Willie McBride staggered to the top of the stand to speak to BBC London and Alun Thomas chatted to Wales before the local Union entertained both teams and guests at the Town Hall in one of the friendliest of reception, highlighted by short speeches and good food, and then back to Arthur's Seat at Capetown and more work before bed, as it was Ascension Day on the morrow and a public holiday. Yet we were able to fly out of Capetown after early morning mist and touch down to a particularly warm reception at Port Elizabeth where two thousand people cheered in the Lions. As at Capetown, such happenings cheer the tourists because it is the people showing their gratitude and not politicians or rugby officials.

The training session was a hard one, watched by old rivals and friends, Amos du Plooy and Ian Kirkpatrick, plus Boete Erasmus (after whom the new ground is named) Lawton Fourie and Jimmy Ward, and there was much amusing banter about previous matches and famous Lions of the past. During the evening the British Press gave 'Big Syd' Millar a birthday party which was much enjoyed, especially the cheerful singing, but as it was a holiday and the dining-rooms and bars closed down early, the situation was saved by Jimmy Ward getting a good supply of South Africa's masterpiece of the culinary arts, the 'toasted sandwich' and, as such, have never tasted as good!

The Lions had another practice on Friday morning when Ken Kennedy had to pull out with a pulled shoulder muscle that proved exceedingly painful at the time, and this brought in Bobby Windsor for his third game in four matches while Gareth Edwards continued at scrum-half and also as captain, as McBride was rested. Sean McKinney and Michael Burton had their first matches of the tour and eight of the side were keen to improve upon their showing at Windhoek.

South Africa's approach to the 'Rugby Ladies' is changing although there are still strong male bastions of refuge and one of the more pleasant is the Port Elizabeth Club. After climbing the hill and chatting with the Club's cheerful secretary about relationships, political and otherwise, it was most enjoyable to take lunch and liquid refreshment with Peter Huggett, an Empire builder from Newport, as host and old friends like Harry O'Connor, the very able editor of the local morning paper, W. I. D. Elliott's cousin and several other friendly types who all asked the same question, not 'Whither South Africa?' but 'Whither Britain?' and I regret I could not answer that one on the day Mrs Williams became a Baroness.

Match No. 4 at Boete Erasmus, Port Elizabeth. May 25, 1974. British Isles defeated Eastern Province by two goals, four penalties and one try (28) to a goal and two tries (14).
Crowd: 30,000. *Weather:* Warm and cloudy. *Ground:* Firm with grass.
Scorers:
British Isles – J. F. Slattery, T. M. Davies and W. C. C. Steele tries, P. Bennett four pens and 2 cons.
Eastern Province – K. Erasmus, D. Campher and J. H. F. Marais tries, G. Cowley one con.

Teams:
BRITISH ISLES: A. R. Irvine; W. C. C. Steele, R. T. G. Bergiers, G. W. Evans, C. Rees, P. Bennett, G. O. Edwards (capt.) J. McLauchlan, R. W. Windsor, M. A. Burton, G. L. Brown, R. M. Uttley, S. A. McKinney, T. M. Davies, J. F. Slattery.
EASTERN PROVINCE: H. van Vuuren; C. Fourie, G. Cowley, D. Campher, F. Meyer; K .Erasmus, F. de Villiers; R. Parker, D. de Coning, J. H. F. Marais (capt.), P. Clarke, T. van der Westhuizen, H. Olwagen, G. Barnard, K. van Eyk.
Referee: Mr F. van der Vyver (Norther Transvaal).

A record crowd for a provincial match at the comparatively new stadium saw the teams take the field, and from the press box right back at the top of the main stand, one has a chess board view of the field and the play. It induced regret for me at not having brought the field glasses from home, although one could not find time to use them and type swiftly for the evening papers. However, such was the happenings of the day that the field glasses would have proved invaluable but Dewi Griffiths, Nigel Starmer-Smith and the South African camera team behind me, did secure a permament record for TV of the unusual happenings on the field of play!

Unfortunately, the Eastern Province were motivated, unwisely I thought, to employ the 'knuckle and stouch', and I still find it difficult to reason why such a calm person as former Springbok centre and member of the 1974 selection committee, Ian Kirkpatrick, was persuaded to allow himself to advise such tactics as coach to the Eastern Province side. Others may have urged him to 'soften up' the Lions but it failed badly and when, in the closing stages, his side decided to run with the ball, they immediately looked dangerous and immeasurably better. A local sports editor of many years experience, Jimmy Hattle, described the side as 'losing its cool', and he was right. They could have done so much better and really challenged the Lions. As it was they reduced their own image and threw away whatever chance they had of achieving the victory they desired.

The Referee, Mr Fonnie van der Vyver of the Northern Transvaal, was just not strong enough to keep the game under control and his approach did neither side a favour, while Gareth Edwards appealed to Hannes Marais as captain of the Eastern Province side to keep more control over the 'wild boys', but Marais more or less hinted that this was not possible, and his three loose forwards continued to 'play up'. Then when the Lions were leading 28–4 late in the second half, the Province suddenly started to run the ball with considerable effect to secure another ten points.

The crowd, naturally, were pleased at the 'grandstand' finish but appeared unhappy with what had gone before and even they realised that, somewhere along the line, the Eastern Province planning had gone wrong unless, of course, the side had been ordered to rough up the Lions a little. That we will never know, although later Hannes Marais denied it, but many South African critics were hard upon the approach of Eastern Province, while the British Press were equally hard and, sadly, it reminded me of the last Cardiff *v.* All Blacks match, when the local club made the same error as Eastern Province, in over-motivating its players.

There were two lessons in the match. First, that British forward play was much stronger and refused to be intimidated, and secondly that when you are on top in South Africa you must not relax but drive home the advantage. When leading 28–4, the Lions should have made it 40–4, and not then played exhibition rugby, even though such Barbarians-type play was much appreciated by the crowd thirsting for open rugby. Little was said in the speeches after the match but the Lions learned much that day that was to help them later.

They took the lead after eight minutes play when the Province sent the ball back from a line-out ten yards from their own line for Erasmus to fumble and Slattery and Davies dive upon the loose ball over the goal line and Slattery to get the touch down for a try that Bennett did not convert. The Province forwards poured through on to Edwards from the line-out, arriving with the ball and cracking him to earth and after a collapsed scrum. The referee did speak to them, but it had little effect, because there followed an open field punch-up between the backs; a rare sight indeed, and this was followed by the first Province try. Erasmus kicked over the Lions goal line and, as the ball rolled to the dead ball line Bennett appeared to be obstructed, and it was Erasmus who got the touch down. The players state that the referee was going to award a penalty to the Lions on their goal line but the Province players spoke to him in Afrikaans.

He then changed his decision and awarded a try which was

not converted, but immediately afterwards Bennett landed a fine 45-yard penalty that just cleared the bar and this was followed by a try from Mervyn Davies after Irvine had launched an attack and kicked on to gather again and feed Davies, on the inside, for him to crash over and Bennett convert. Before the interval Province were penalised for offside play and Bennett kicked a 27-yard goal to make it 16–4 and another day for the Lions. Edwards was the victim of all kinds of tackles and one felt that some of his opponents were trying to put him on the touch line. They did so for a few minutes, while he recovered from one severe and unnecessary tackle, but he was soon back again, playing as well as ever.

Another fierce punch-up followed early in the second half and it ended with McKinney running across to the scene of the outbreak and 'flooring' the troublesome Van Eyk with a left cross. This was unlike the pleasant flanker but, obviously, he had seen enough to warrant such drastic action which could have found him ordered from the field, but the referee was many yards away and, apparently, undisturbed by the happenings. Maybe he wasn't too distressed, for minutes later there was a flash of good rugby from the Lions. They moved the ball to the left and then Bennett, running well, switched to the right and along the line it went. A brief halt and Bergiers fed Steele who cut inside cleverly to score. Bennett kicked a superb goal from far out and another penalty when Irvine, on the attack, was late tackled. The Lions attacked superbly now and almost crossed on two occasions before further offside play by Province brought Bennett his fourth penalty, this time from 22 yards.

At 28–4, the Lions should have pursued their relentless attacks, but they appeared to ease a little, realising the match was won. Back came the Province side running the ball. They got a good try through Campher which Cowley converted and then one from a short penalty although the move appeared halted near the left corner, Marais picked up and scored and the match ended at 28–14. It was a triumph for the Lions forwards and halves, and all five Springbok selectors watched the match before moving over to the Hotel Elizabeth, the latest in the modern American Hilton-type hotels in the city, to nominate their trial teams. There was a brief reception at which Hannes Maris asked John Reason, Terry O'Connor and myself, to allow the Lions to get on and play rugby. This was difficult to understand because we wished them to do so, or did he fear that we would criticise the match?

Every British pressman present at the match did so. I said on the BBC that it was more disappointing than sensational, in that Eastern Province tried to intimidate the Lions and failed, and this point must have been appreciated by Eastern Province as Hannes Marais was reported to have said afterwards, 'The Springboks will have to think of other ways than through the forwards to beat the Lions.' There followed a good party in the evening at the Marine Hotel and the Eastern Province Union headed by Lawton Fourie, Jimmy Ward and press liaison officer Manny Katze lacked nothing in hospitality, even if the playing side of their Union had gone astray.

Slattery suffered a knock on the knee, Edwards a bad back and near the end a Province forward stamped on Bobby Windsor's ankle, an injury that was to worry him later and upset the Lions selection plans. Sunday was a free day, but many of those Lions who went fishing in the morning 'suffered' badly and fed many more fishes than they caught. Most disturbed was expert river fisherman Gareth Edwards, who pleaded with the boat's skipper to turn and head for the shore. Windsor was ready to dive over the side before the boat was finally secured along side and several pale-faced Lions proceeded to their hotel, much the worse for wear. The moral of it all was – never go fishing after a rugby 'night out' unless you have sea legs! Tom David was the only successful angler.

The next day there was an early start for the Press party and one of the best days of the tour, the first of relaxation. Everyone got his copy away early and then proceeded by coach from Port Elizabeth to Mossel Baai along the Garden Route, and wonderful it was. Readers may not appreciate that for journalists with a touring party, it is a seven day week at work, as it is for the Manager and coach, and a 'day for the Queen' now and again works wonders. After stopping at various gorges to take pictures the party had a superb picnic lunch at Nature's Valley Bay on top of a giant rock on the sands as the breakers rolled in magnificently, the water glistening in the sun. A Press team picture was taken and later, at Wilderness, an impromptu game of soccer between the South African and British press was played on the sands, without a referee. The South African Press claimed a victory and the 'Britse Pers' captain let in a last-minute goal believing his side was leading two nil! Then a few songs 'on the road' before the coach reached Mossel Baai. A good time had been had by all, a cliché perhaps but, in this case, a true one. The tour was really on the road!

Match No. 5 at Van Riebeck Stadium Mossel Baai. May 29 1974.
British Isles defeated South West Districts by 15 goals, one penalty and one try (97) to nil (0).
Crowd: 7,000 *Weather:* Dry after rain. *Ground:* Yielding with grass.
Scorers:
British Isles – J. J. Williams(6), G. Evans(3), J. P. R. Williams(2), T. Grace, A. G. Old, J. J. Maloney, J .F. Slattery and T. M. Davies tries. A. G. Old 15 cons and 1 pen.
Teams:
SOUTH WEST DISTRICTS: D. Pienaar; A. Du Toit, S. de Lange, J. Botes, A. van Tonder; M. van der Westhuizen, J. Taljaart; L. Swart (capt.), J. Blom, J. Gerber, S. Van der Menwe, J. le Grange, D. du Toit, S. Jonker, H. du Toit.
BRITISH ISLES: A. R. Irvine; T. O. Grace, G. W. Evans, R. A. Milliken, J. J. Williams; A. G. B. Old, J. J. Maloney; M. A. Burton, K. W. Kennedy, F. E. Cotton, W. J. McBride (capt.), C. W. Ralston, J. F. Slattery, T. M. Davies, S. A. McKinney.
Replacement: J. P. R. Williams for Grace after 20 mins second half.
Referee: Mr Max Baise (Western Province).

It had to happen somewhere, sometime, that a Lions side would play for 80 minutes as a well-drilled machine, never faltering or stopping in a relentless pursuit of points while demonstrating all the fine arts of rugby. This was the day; May 29, 1974, with McBride and his merry men the heroes and poor South West Districts the victims, although they were not 'baddies' in this admirable display of quality. Although outpaced, out-thought and beaten badly for possession, they played in the true spirit of the game, never once raising the finger or the leg to impede the rampaging British unfairly, and in this they set an excellent example to all sides.

The captain of the SW Districts XV told his team before they took the field, 'If we can contain the Lions score to under 100, we will achieve a moral victory!' They did so but, only just, for when the final whistle was blown, the Lions had reached 97, the highest in their history, the highest by any touring side in South Africa, and only two points short of the highest total in a first class match in South Africa.

Alan Old, at outside-half, enjoyed an historic day by scoring 37 points, the highest tally by any Lion in any land, the highest score by any player in South Africa, and only four short of the world's record set up some weeks previously by Joe Karam of New Zealand in Australia!

The Lions tally of 16 tries was the highest by them in any land while John J. Williams, with six of them, equalled the Lions record created by David Duckham in New Zealand in 1971, and passing the previous best in South Africa of five by W. Wallace of the 1924 side. It was a fine feat as the wing had not scored previously on the tour and admitted, 'This is a tremendous boost for my confidence!' It was, and to be bracketed with Duckham at the top of the list made him very happy. In Llanelli they were pleased and many extra copies of the *Western Mail* were sold the next morning.

With all these records falling it was quite a day. Dr Danie Craven said the next day that his Board would have to look into the question of touring teams playing against the weaker Provinces. He should think again! The crowd loved it; the South West side was not disgraced, and it was the SA Board who divided up the major provinces into smaller units to help rugby. Thus it follows that top touring sides should play everywhere to promulgate the game and, before the start of the tour, the Lions had agreed to change two of the weaker fixtures, at Upington and Craddock, where they would have enjoyed staying. It was pleasantly relaxing at Mossel Baai for all, and any touring team is entitled to such a break.

The play of the Lions was superb. They scrummaged well; jumped strongly at the line-out where Chris Ralston came back to form, foraged in the loose and won most of the ball at rucks and mauls. McBride had them going together as a unit and John Maloney, whose appearance was something of a gamble following his shoulder injury, had a smooth effective match and Alan Old, obviously, had the best and most successful match of his career. Thus all four half-backs were fit again and in top form.

The three-quarters ran quickly and elusively, and handled with amazing accuracy. Tom Grace left the field with a badly bruised shoulder after 20 minutes of the second and Andy Irvine, playing with much more confidence, moved to the wing, J. P. R. Williams taking over at full-back, to help himself to two tries. At half time it was 37–0 before the Lions collected 60 points in an amazing second half, when even the members of the press and radio boxes were overcome by figures and the broken records. It was wonderful stuff; Lions rugby at its very best, and the modest Syd Millar commented, 'I am satisfied now that we are making the right progress. Everyone is going forward and not wasting possession as we did at one stage at Port Elizabeth.' A perfectionist and a wise one.

There was a quiet celebration in the evening following a happy reception for both sides where President Powell delivered an oration to the players and guests that would have been admired by the late Sir Williams Ramsay and such was its length, power and good humour, that the Lions' manager and captain could hardly say more than genuine 'Thank you!' Pressman Chris Lander experienced a frustrating evening being unable to make contact with friends and Nigel Starmer-Smith was beguiled by the gentle folk of upper Mossel Baai, while Pippa and Nelles Vincent and their friends cared for the 'Britse Pers'. In the morning when some heads were heavy through lack of sleep but happy with the records of the previous day still buzzing in them, the Press party set off for George to fly to Capetown by 'Dak' while the Lions drove to Cudtshoorn to train, have a barbecue and visit the Cango Caves before flying back to Capetown in two 'Daks'.

At George Airport, the Press and Radio party had one of its happiest hours on the tour. Chris Lander and Colm Smith were in tremendous form, as Kingsford Lander and Wiley Smith the world's two most famous aviators who acted as stewards and really 'got the Dak in the air with the aid of a cycle which they both road at the same time', while Nigel Starmer-Smith was a fireman first-class and an able stewardess who brewed tea and coffee in the tiny lounge of the airport! In all fairness it was the smallest and friendliest airport any Lions press party had visited, and the faithful Dak got us all to the Cape on time! So ended the 'honeymoon', as the serious stuff was now ahead of the Lions, with four matches in the city. If all could be won, the Lions would have 'made' their tour and the atmosphere was charged with friendly challenge, for Capetown is a gentle place, but the players of the Western Province are good, sometimes very good!

CHAPTER FIVE

The First Test

On arrival in Cape Town the Lions selectors announced their shadow Test XV to do duty against Western Province. It comprised six Welshmen, five Scots, two Irish and two Englishmen and, if not the strongest available, it was a strong one nevertheless, and expected to beat the Province despite the fact that the local side contained many good players, was playing well, and was excellently coached. However, the match had a vital bearing upon the test match due to be played seven days later and the enthusiasm for it in the city was considerable.

Capetonians have a pride in the Western Province side with its long history of open play and production of Springbok backs. They support a side that plays good rugby and there is nothing they enjoy more than a match with the British Lions. This may well be due to the fact that there are almost as many people of British descent in the Cape Province as there are in Natal. Few said that Western Province would beat the Lions but they all said that they would give the tourists a game to remember, good and hard!

This they did; make no mistake about it, and the Lions will remember it, but let me start at the beginning as, soon after arrival at the friendly and well-appointed Arthur's Seat Hotel, I was whisked away to the Dinner of the Western Province Referees Association to deputise for Alun Thomas, otherwise engaged genuinely with affairs of state. Young Andy Irvine and John Maloney travelled with me to a new hotel near Newlands and my old friend, and a fine referee during the 1955 tour, Ralph Burmister, was in the chair as the Association's president. It was a most enjoyable evening and lots of stories (fact not fiction) about happenings on the rugby field that appeared to amuse the guests, and the two players and myself were cordially received and extremely well treated.

The next day the tourists paid their first visit of the tour to Newlands and although it was raining one felt the atmosphere of the ground and admired the new stands. It looked a completed ground at last. Pete Lombard, the Western Province secretary, and his staff were as helpful as ever and the stage was set for the big match.

Following their record breaking display at Mossel Baai the Lions were big news and the two excellent local English language newspapers, the *Cape Argus* and the *Cape Times*, gave considerable space to the Lions arrival, training, off-the-field activities and, of course, the preview. So much so, that one felt it was Cardiff and not Cape Town, except that it was the Arthur's Seat Hotel and not the Angel, and the giant Atlantic waves were pounding the shore. The pouring rain was similar, and a chat with Alun Thomas after breakfast reminded me of the Angel for he was keen, determined and courteous but admitted, 'We must win this one!'

Life on tour is like that, always, for one moves from match to match, hoping that the victories will continue. Perhaps in 1971 it was slightly different, as one got into the habit of thinking that the side could not lose and, as it lost only once more after the first match at Brisbane, it is easy to see why one acquired that state of mind. In 1974, it was slightly different and it was after this match that one felt it could be just the same, and one does not write this without a great deal of thought and genuine comparison.

The International Board members flew in from Australia to watch three important matches of the tour, against Western Province, the Proteas and the First Test, and Harry McKibbin, Kenneth Harris, Charles Drummond and Dudley Kemp were soon settled in. Alun Thomas and Syd Millar, chaperoned by former 1938 Lion, Jeff Reynolds, paid a courtesy call upon the 'Board' and brought everyone up to date on the tour. The Management had no complaints but we wondered how much the Board had accomplished at its Sydney Meeting.

One deplored the change to the metric system because the '25', lines were very much part of the game's tradition, as was the Ground's length of 110 yards. Secondly, attention was drawn to Law 19 and Law 23, and it was on the line-out trouble that they held firm, ignoring the claim that it was 'instinctive' for a player to move towards the ball. However, they asked all member Unions to keep statistics in relation to infringements so that existing penalty awards may be reviewed and consideration given to the case for differential and indirect penalties. A good thing this; much needed in the game, which is fast becoming a kicker's paradise.

Match No. 6, at Newlands, Capetown. Saturday, June 1, 1974.
British Isles beat Western Province by three penalties and two tries (17) to two tries (8).
Crowd: 45,000. *Weather:* Sunny. *Ground:* Softish – drying out.
Scorers:
British Isles – C. Rees and G. L. Brown tries. P. Bennett three pens.
Western Province – A. Read (2) tries.
Teams:
WESTERN PROVINCE – J. Brink; A. Read, P. Whipp, J. Oosthuizen, C. Pope, D. Snyman, R. McCallum, R. Bryant, R. Cockrell, D. Claxton, J. Immelman, P. du Plessis, J. Coetzee, D. MacDonald, M. du Plessis (capt).
BRITISH ISLES – J. P. R. Williams; C. Rees, I. R. McGeechan, R. T. E. Bergiers, W. C. C. Steele; P. Bennett, G. O. Edwards; J. McLauchlan, R. W. Windsor, A. B. Carmichael, G. L. Brown, W. J. McBride (capt), S. A. McKinney, A. G. Ripley, A. Neary.
Referee: I. Gourlay (Natal).

Western Province officials expected 40,000 spectators but the weather showed a considerable improvement during the morning and when the teams fielded there were 45,000 packed into the historic Newlands Ground, and I sat with my 'hot line' to the *Echo* in Cardiff at my side in the Press Box, wondering whether I would be able to hear them above the noise of an excited crowd. It was never easy since the match proved a desparately exciting one, with first the Lions on top for 20 minutes and then the Province getting back into the match and challenging strongly, before the Lions made the match safe in the closing stages.

It was a repeat of many previous exciting matches at the ground in which the Lions have been involved and not unlike the 1962 match, although in this latest one the Province did not actually get into the lead. Yet they played with tremendous spirit and skill and, at times, rocked the Lions back on their heels, as the loose forwards and mid-field backs gave it a 'whirl' by running and handling cleverly. At times the Lions defences were breached, only for two senior players, John Williams at full-back and Gareth Edwards at scrum-half, to hold fast against the attacking tide.

But for them the Lions could have lost the match, although the winning margin was three penalty goals by Phil Bennett as each side scored two tries.

For once, Bennett was not as accurate as usual, kicking only three goals in nine attempts, and this was due I believe to the fact that his left foot was not as firm as normally on the soft Newlands surface which, unfortunately, was far below test standard. Bennett slipped attempting his first kick, the conversion of Rees's try, and it was some time before his rhythm returned, although his last kick was a superb effort from the touch line. At this stage the Lions were leading by 14–8, and a goal by Western Province would have made it 14–14 with five minutes left for play, and then there would have been even more excitement. However, Bennett, from the right touch line, put over a beauty and that was that, but the Lions had been chased hard and, as such, it was an excellent exercise following the 97–0 affair.

In the first twenty minutes the Lions forwards played superbly well to get an 11 point lead. It was started after four minutes when Bennett put up a high attacking punt to the right where Oosthuizen gathered and then attempted to find touch on the other side of the field. Rees gathered, with a juggle in full flight, and went on to cross for a try that Bennett, through slipping, failed to convert from a wide angle. Five minutes later he found a firm spot and banged over a 30 yard penalty when the Province were penalised at a set scrum for 'not straight'.

The Lions forwards continued to exert pressure and hammered away to start one thinking about a big victory. Bennett kicked wide from the near touch-line with two penalty attempts and, from the second drop out by the Province high up mid-field, John Williams gathered at full-back and raced away on the best run of the match, swerving and side stepping and beating at least five opponents to get deep into the Province '25'. There he found Gordon Brown up with him on his right to take the scoring pass and dive over but Bennett was again wide with the conversion.

Still, with a lead of 11 points the Lions appeared to be moving along smoothly to a comfortably victory, before Western Province suddenly thrust deep into enemy territory and scored to change the whole pattern of the game. Snyman was wide with a penalty attempt and then they forced their way down to the Lions '25' for a line-out on their right. They peeled smartly from the line-out, won the ruck outside the posts before moving the ball smartly to the left, for Reed on the wing to score in the corner. Snyman failed with the conversion and then with two reasonable penalty attempts before full-back Brink failed with another.

At the interval it was 11–4 to the Lions but, as the crowd buzzed in conversation, one realised that there were high hopes that the Province would topple the Lions and for the first twenty minutes of the second spell it was fast and exciting. The challenge was on and the Western Province trio of loose forwards did not spare themselves. Bennett kicked wide with a couple of penalty attempts and had these gone over then, perhaps, the effort of the Province would have weakened a little. Williams and Edwards were magnificent heroes with their aggressive defence and perfect temperament under pressure. I have never seen Williams play better than he did in this match and his standard is always high, while Edwards was superb.

After 20 minutes Edwards made one of his irrepressible touch-line dashes and eventually crossed the line in the right corner only for the touch judge to correctly assess that he had put a heel on the touch line. This try would have settled it there and then, but Province pegged away and after 30 minutes got another try which really increased the tension. From a loose ruck Morne du Plessis set off and Roy McCallum made the decisive break before handing on to MacDonald, a most useful ball carrier, and finally a long pass to Read, steaming up on the left. He juggled dangerously but just held the ball and was over in the corner. Snyman could not convert it but another goal would have brought the Province level. They tried hard but Williams and Edwards were in no mood to concede the prize and three minutes from the end Brink was caught in possession and not able to play the ball near the touch-line. A penalty was awarded and Bennett kicked the goal to seal the fate of a brave and attractive Province side that had upheld the glorious past.

Morne du Plessis and Willie McBride spoke exceedingly well after the match and du Plessis said, 'Boy Louw came into the dressing room before the start and told us, "I wish I was coming out with you to play today!" and it helped us to go on and play hard in a great match.' He was right, it was a splendid match with a little of each of the qualities that go to make a real rugby game. The crowd loved it and the critics had plenty to write about. The

Lions had readjusted quickly. They knew after this what 'life at the top' in South African rugby was all about, at least on the field of play if not along the corridors of power.

The good folks at home were taken aback, at least a little, when the Sunday papers carried a warning note in their pages, that the Lions faced a formidable task in the series, while suggesting there were certain weaknesses in the side, particularly in midfield defence. A happy evening was enjoyed at the hotel and then much furious typing of cables on Sunday before a pleasant ride along the beaches of the Cape and a quiet meal that included some of the best beef steak tasted in Southern Africa. The next match was that against the coloured Proteas team and eyes and ears were alerted on Monday for action.

The Lions visited the University of the Southern Cape for coloured students and much enjoyed their outing. Vivian Jenkins arrived in the evening to complete the Press corps and bring news from home with messages for many 'on the road', while at dinner the players stood as Vivian entered the dining-room as a mark of respect to the senior traveller!

The next day saw the Press party visit the Goodwood Showground Stadium for the match and the temperature was not far short of that experienced at Wellington for the Boland match. In other words it was too d . . . . hot for rugby! Fergus Slattery was given command of the Lions side in the absence of both McBride and Edwards and, as the teams entered the field a few minutes after 3.30 p.m., a Press Box 'wag' suggested it was due to the length of Slattery's team talk. Twenty thousand spectators were there in the public stadium with far more coloureds than whites and they cheered lustily. Normally, the coloureds in Cape Town, who are among the most knowledgeable of rugby followers, cheer for the Lions, but this time they were cheering for their own side. It was an historic occasion; the first time a British Lions side had played against anything other than an all European side in South Africa, but it was also to be a sad one in that it cost the Lions the services of one of their most useful players and an ideal tourist in Alan Old.

Match No. 7, at Goodwood Stadium, Capetown. June 4, 1974. British Isles beat Proteas by one goal, five penalties and four tries (37) to one dropped goal and one penalty (6).

Crowd: 20,000. *Weather:* Warm and sunny. *Ground:* Hard with grass.
Scorers:
British Isles – J. F. Slattery, G. L. Brown, R. Bergiers, J. J Williams, R. Milliken tries, A. G. Old two penalties, A. Irvine three penalties, one conversion.
Proteas – E. Tobias one dropped goal and one penalty.
Teams:
PROTEAS: E. Frans; E. Wildermans, C. Cupido, H. Shields, J. Noble; E. Tobias, A. Lategan; H. Shields, C. Davids, D. Dyers, (Capt) T. Petersen, J. Smith, J. Meyer, J. Juries, J. Mawson.
BRITISH ISLES: A. Irvine; T. O. Grace, G. W. Evans, R. A. Milliken, J. J. Williams; A. G. B. Old, J. J. Moloney; F. E. Cotton, K. Kennedy, M. Burton G. L. Brown, C.W. Ralston, R. M. Uttley, T. M. Davies, J. F. Slattery (capt).
Referee: D. Katzenellenbogen (Western Province)

This was a most unusual match and in all my travels I have never seen one quite like it at representative level. It was unbounded and uncontrolled enthusiasm on the part of the Proteas and remarkable restraint on the part of the Lions, yet it cost the tourists the services of an invaluable player in Alan Old who, in a late tackle, long after the ball had gone, suffered a torn medial cartilage at the back of his knee. This happened during the first half and a second tackle forced him to leave the field after 20 minutes and be removed to hospital, where an operation was performed the next day and his leg put in plaster to rule him out of the tour.

Syd Millar was beside himself with anger at the injury but contained himself and did not burst upon the referee, who was strangely casual and inadequate for such an occasion and was, in the main, responsible for much uncontrolled late tackling and offside play that made it extremely difficult for the Lions to produce a normal style of play. They won comfortably enough in the end and although they had every intention of helping the coloured players, they did not enjoy the match, for the referee did not help either side by his obvious lack of strictness.

One sensed that the Proteas must play with a lack of control and sense of discipline in their own matches and this was increased by the incentive to do well against the Lions in a match receiving maximum publicity and TV and Radio coverage. They were over-motivated and this did not help but even at the risk of blowing all too frequently, it would have been much more valuable for the Proteas to have enjoyed fairly strict refereeing, which would have indicated to them and their followers what is required in first-class rugby.

The sight of scrum-half John Moloney waiting for the ball to emerge from scrum and ruck with a Protea player on either side of him was not amusing and if Moloney did get it away, the ball reached Milliken at deputy outside-half, since Roy Bergiers replaced the injured Old and played in the centre, accompanied by two Proteas. All this helped to disturb the rhythm of the Lions backs and allowed little chance for the players fighting for a place in the Test XV to reveal their best form.

In the first half the Lions, to put it mildly, were struggling and at half-time led by only 13–6. Old put them in the lead with a penalty and Tobias, a lively outside half, levelled for the Proteas with a dropped goal. Old regained the lead with a second penalty before Slattery got the first try. Another penalty goal was kicked by Irvine followed by one from Tobias and it was 13–6 before Brown dived over smartly from a line-out early in the second half and made it 17–6 and Irvine kicked his second penalty for 20–6.

In the last 20 minutes of play the Lions collected another 17 points with tries by Bergiers, Williams and Milliken. Irvine converted one and kicked another penalty and it was 37–6 at the end, but one felt it had not done a great deal of good for the coloureds. Their Federation represented a small group of clubs as compared with the other coloured Union which has many more clubs and players. A dinner followed at Goodwood and the Lions returned to face three days preparation for the First Test, which was the match the tourists really wanted to win. The honeymoon, however hard, was over and the Lions awaited eagerly the selection of the test XV which was made the next day and, inevitably, certain players had to be disappointed.

On the Tuesday of the Proteas match, the South African selectors held their final trial at Newlands and then spent many hours picking their test side which was announced late at night. It was based on the Western Province side, seven of whom were included, and there were two brothers in full-back Ian McCallum and scrum-half Roy, the first pair since the Bekkers of 1953. Six of the players were new caps and Keven de Klerk, a lock, became the 101st player to represent South Africa from the Transvaal.

The Lions brought in Fran Cotton to the front row instead of Sandy Carmichael and fielded a back row of Fergus Slattery and Roger Uttley on the flanks with Mervyn Davies at No. 8. At three-quarter Billy Steele and John J. Williams won the wing positions and Dick Milliken and Ian McGeechan were at centre. Obviously, Tony Neary, who had never been dropped by England, Sandy Carmichael who missed a test place through injury in New Zealand and Roy Bergiers who started the tour as first choice centre, were all disappointed. Yet, as McBride told me, 'There are always players who have to be disappointed but they get over it in a couple of days, once they have played again.'

The Springboks trained mainly in secret but that did not worry the British Press in any way while the Lions had two good sessions, one in Cape Town and one at Stellenbosch which was not attended by the British press, although there were two anonymous South African pressmen hiding behind trees and 'spotting' for the Springboks. However, their reports did not influence the result!

The weather started to break up as Saturday neared and Syd Millar gave the final team talk on Friday night after the players watched Dewi 'Quo Vardis' Griffith's presentation of BBC TV's film of the Eastern Province match at the team hotel, before handing over to McBride who was responsible for the final motivation. One sensed the tension increasing with the passing of each hour and on Saturday morning the hotel was truly affected by the test match atmosphere that only a Lions tour can produce. The two main Cape newspapers were full of articles, pictures and records to motivate the spectators but Saturday morning was wet and, with the thought of two curtain raisers not being cancelled, the prospect was for a mud pie ground that would be less friendly for the Springboks than it was for the Lions. Why, oh why play curtain raisers on wet days? Bring the kick off time forward and open the gates later, then there would be no need to entertain spectators admitted too early and protect the ground from over use as no test ground in a rain area gets as much use as Newlands.

On arriving at Newlands and sighting the pitch while the final curtain raiser was in progress, International Board member Ronnie Dawson of Ireland, really let 'go' to me privately, and one had to agree with his views that it was nonsense to endanger the quality of the play in the test match by such matches, even if the crowd became restive without them. The spectators had come to see the test and paid good money to do so, much more than they would in the British Isles, and really it was the 'TEST' and nothing else that mattered. The Press Box was full and there was hardly enough room for the Lions replacements and coach Millar alongside but, eventually, they were accommodated and the teams fielded to loud cheering and waving of banners. The great moment had arrived.

Match No. 8. The First Test at Newlands, Cape Town. Saturday, June 8, 1974.
British Isles defeated South Africa by three penalties and one dropped goal (12) to one dropped goal (3).
Crowd: 42,700. *Weather:* Dry after rain. *Ground:* Wet and muddy.
Scorers:
British Isles – P. Bennett three pens. G. O. Edwards one dropped goal.
South Africa – D. Snyman one dropped goal.
Teams:
SOUTH AFRICA: I. McCallum (N); G. Muller (T), P. Whipp J. Oosthuizen (WP), A. Read (WP); D. Snyman (WP), R. MacCallum (WP); J. Sauerman (T), J. Van Wyk (NT) J. H. F. Marais (EP) capt.) J. Williams (NT), K. de Kerk(T), J. Coetzee (WP), M. du Plessis (WP), J. Ellis (SWA)
BRITISH ISLES: J. P. R. Williams (W); J. J. Williams (W), R. A. Milliken (I), I. R. McGeechan (S), W. C. C. Steele (S); P. Bennett (W), G. O. Edwards (W); J. McLauchlan (S), R. W. Windsor (W), F. E. Cotton (E), G. L. Brown (S), W. J. McBride (capt.) (I), R. M. Uttley (E), T. M. Davies (W), J. F. Slattery (I).
Referee: Mr M. Baise (South Africa)

The Springboks won the toss and Hannes Marais decided to play with the wind which, apparently, was contrary to tradition at Newlands, and there were some members of the Press Box who saw this as an unhappy omen. Phil Bennett started the match, kicking to his left, and with the ball in the air the 1974

Test series was under way. The Springboks were awarded the first penalty and then two to the Lions before the fourth kick provided Ian McCallum with a 67 yard attempt that fell well short.

Both sides tested each other with high kicks and Snyman probed across field for South Africa while Edwards dropped short punts into the 'box' for J. J. Williams to run on to, and one was extremely near a score as the ball and the wing slid into touch in goal. The Springboks enjoyed some good line-out ball at this stage but the Lions were noticibly much more comfortable in the set scrum and surprisingly quick to the loose ball on the muddy, tacky surface. Twice the Lions had to drop out after the ball had gone dead while, at the other end, McCallum at full-back effected some excellent catches and clearances.

After 20 minutes of play, it was fairly obvious that there would not be much in it although the longer the Lions held out against the wind, the better it would be for them. Three minutes later the Springboks took the lead. They were awarded a penalty kick just inside the Lions half after a scrum offence and Ian McCallum attempted a 52 yard goal, but the ball sailed wide and J. J. Williams, attempting a clearing kick, only found touch in goal. A scrum five was ordered and the Springboks won the ball and moved away before a ruck was set up, and from it the ball went back again to Snyman, who dropped a quick goal and put South Africa in the lead.

The challenge was on and the Lions had to hold and contain until the interval. John Williams made a fine clearance. Mervyn Davies was hurt and had to have attention. Edwards was everywhere and Bennett tremendously cool and confident. The three-quarters stood their ground in defence and covered the kicks while the pack gradually got the measure of the Springbok eight. No drive developed and the back row of Slattery, Davies and Uttley allowed nothing to move across the advantage line in a defensive web that disturbed the Springboks. After 34 minutes the Springbok backs fell offside at a line-out, inside their own '25', and Phil Bennett, kicking from 22 yards landed the goal that brought the Lions level and, from that moment onwards, the result was never in doubt. The Lions forwards improved in all phases of the play. They scrummaged well, turning it at will to give Edwards the best feed. They held their own at the line-out and started winning better ball more frequently. They were getting more rucked and mauled ball and South Africa's possession grew less in quantity and poorer in quality. One could hardly believe the measure of control the Lions forwards produced in their containment of the Springbok pack, expected beforehand to take control and set the Western Province backs running.

Edwards was kicking superbly, tantalisingly, and low and accurately along the ground with top spin to drive the Springboks forwards back and back, and set their backs on their heels, unable to launch attacks. When the interval arrived with the score level at three points apiece, the match, virtually, had been decided, and it remained for the Lions to consolidate their position with the wind behind them. There was no trouble in the tight as the front row of McLauchlan, Windsor and Cotton was comfortable and effective and it won the tight head strike in the end by 3–2, which gave Windsor enormous pleasure. 'They were calling for more weight,' he told me afterwards, 'and Fran Cotton was extremely strong and effective while the Mighty Mouse had all the answers. I was very comfortable there and enjoyed every minute of it.'

The 'father and son' combination at lock, McBride and his protegé Brown, grew in stature and stamina as the match progressed, and McBride at 34 years of age was as good as any of his pack, while Mervyn Davies has never played better. One tackle on Jan Ellis in the second half was a 'cruncher', and symbolic of the Lions' controlled forward strength, while the co-ordination between forwards and halves was quite uncanny and the whole effort was impressive, more so than in any Test in New Zealand in 1971. It warmed the heart to see the Lions play so well; to employ the basics of forward play so effectively; to support each other in attack and defence like a well oiled machine and, for Thomas and Millar in the stand, it was a moment to savour.

After four minutes of the second half the Springboks fell offside on the wrong side of a maul and Phil Bennett from 30 yards banged over a lovely goal from near the touch line, with the ball dipping over the bar and the touch judges' flags shooting skywards to put the Lions into the lead. It was 20 minutes before they scored again and again it was a 30 yard penalty from Phil Bennett from near the touch line, when Roy McCallum was adjudged offside at a scrum after the ball was out, and one could debate whether the ball rebounded from a Lion. Now it was 9–3 and only a converted breakaway try could bring the Springboks level and they would have to score twice to regain the lead.

Five minutes later came the decisive score. The Lions moved into the attack and Davies set up a ruck 30 yards out from the Springboks line where the ball came back smartly and cleanly to Edwards who, without the slightest hesitation, lined up the posts and dropped for goal. Instead of kicking in an arc, he kicked straight and the ball flew high between the posts. Referee Baise pointed to the halfway line; the Coloured spectators in their stand had seen it clearly and cheered loudly, and the Springboks lined up for the restart with 10 minutes left for play, a beaten and contained side.

Yet play remained clean if hard, without any incident, although we did not appreciate at the time that Springbok centre, Johaan Oosthuizen, had suffered a cracked cheek bone in making a save and being rucked since there was no stoppage to indicate such a happening, and this was to keep him out of the South African side for the rest of the series. The minutes ticked away; Edwards made his characteristic end of the match charge, knocking down a couple of forwards, and when the final whistle sounded the Lions jumped high into the air. A precious victory, indeed!

They trotted off with arms held high; delighted with their deserved success, and the moment of truth had proved them a worthy Lions side, well fitted to follow in the footsteps of the 1971 team. On the day, and this is always important, the 1974 pack was better than any one fielded in 1971. Again, the halves were just as effective as in 1971, since Edwards was the controller as was Barry John previously, and Phil Bennett his most devoted and confident assistant. The Springboks just could not get at these two Welsh 'aces', with the Lions forwards in control and providing a launching platform as wide as the bridge of the QE2.

The Springboks pack disappointed and it was but a mere shadow of the great packs of ten years previously and before that. Marais could not inspire them and the back row men were tied to the scrums and mauls in defence, unable to roam. The long legged men of the highveld found the sticky Newlands turf demanding and tiring. Even Jan Ellis met his match in the battle of the 'fringes' and he was a shadow of the marauder that worried the Lions at Windhoek. Roy McCallum and Dawie Synman at half-back were on their heels for most of the match and the three-quarter line did not move in unison until an hour had elapsed, while Ian McCallum at full-back had a lot of work to do in defence which he did well, but he could not shine in attack or as a place kicker.

For Willie John McBride it was a memorable day; probably the greatest of his career, as he led a Lions side to victory in a test at Newlands for the first time in 36 years, and followed his Irish predecessors, Sam Walker and Robin Thompson into history. It was 19 years since the Lions had even won a test in South Africa and McBride deserved every line of praise that was written about him in generous South African newspapers. His pack played superbly and clustered round him to earn Dr Danie Craven's accolade . . . 'you could have covered them with a blanket . . . without possession of the ball you cannot control a game . . . the Lions won good possession throughout.'

One up and three to play was a happy position, even if there were harder matches ahead, especially on the highveld, but the side was on top of the world. Edwards told me he had never felt better at any time in his career and, as an observer, I had never seen him play better in a big match. He was the 'master' and South African critics readily greeted him as the greatest of scrum-halves. Yet Edwards is a shrewd sportsman and realised that in the eyes of the public you are only as good as your last match. It would be difficult for him to improve upon this one!

For Syd Millar it was a moment of supreme satisfaction as a coach who had prepared a pack to contain a Springbok eight on its own territory, while for manager Thomas the day had a special significance as ten years previously he had seen Wales hammered by South Africa at Durban and, as he watched, he said to himself, 'This is not good enough, we must change our whole approach and get on terms with these people.' On this day the Lions got on top and it was a triumph for British coaching methods, in the schools, in the clubs, in the counties, and in the countries,

Saturday night provided a happy party, although visitors at 2.30 a.m. Sunday morning were a reminder of the great days of New Zealand 1971. This was the first triumph and there had to be others before one could 'empty the bottle'. Sunday was a day of complete relaxation for the team; all deserved it and even the Manager cast aside the cares he had shouldered since joining the side in London. On Monday morning there were a few 'sore' heads but the Millar Man was out on the training field and it was back to work in the pouring rain before being entertained by the first citizen of Cape Town at the City Hall. It is so pleasant on tour when your side is winning and these Lions were starting to assume a special image and appear extremely formidable. So much so that many in South Africa were shaken and unduly pessimistic.

Yet the rain kept falling in Cape Town; nothing could stop its steady flow and the historic Newlands Ground remained a quagmire. On Monday night it rained even harder, and by Tuesday morning, Newlands was a lake, grim and uninviting. Would they cancel the curtain raiser? Not on your 'nelly', and this was more unfortunate for the Combined Southern Universities side than it was for the Lions since whatever hope the students had of winning was through running the ball and not in confrontation with the Lions forwards.

In the British Isles there are no curtain raisers and in good weather they are more than useful in entertaining the waiting test or big match crowds but, on wet days and we had three of them at Newlands, they went on and on to create quagmires. Tradition dies hard but this tradition did no good for Western Province rugby. When we arrived at Newlands and saw the curtain raiser being played on a waterlogged field we were amazed, but one thing was certain, Morne du Plessis and his mixed band of students, past and present, and tradesmen would never win in the bog that was Newlands. It was as simple as that . . . they never had a chance, whereas in dry weather they could have come near to 1955, one of the great matches at Newlands, between the same teams.

Match No. 9, at Newlands, Cape Town. Tuesday, June 11, 1974.
British Isles defeated Southern Universities by two goals, two penalties and four tries (26) to a try (4).
Crowd: 20,000. *Weather:* Raining. *Ground:* Quagmire.
Scorers:
British Isles – Bergiers, Brown, Uttley, Brown (push over) tries, Irvine two cons and two pens.

Above: The 3rd test at Port Elizabeth, 13th July. Gordon Brown scores the first try for the Lions from a line-out in injury time in the first half (*Basil Hall, Eastern Province Herald*).

Below: The 3rd test. Gareth Edwards sends his line away (*John Rubython*).

Above: The series is won! The three architects of victory, Willie John McBride, Gareth Edwards and coach Syd Millar celebrate in the dressing-room after the 3rd test (*John Rubython*).

Left: The white hunters! Bobby Windsor and Ian McLauchlan after 'bagging' a Springbok on Safari near Kimberley (*John Rubython*).

Ambition fulfilled! Gordon Brown plays golf in Johannesburg with British Open winner Gary Player (*Gert Hattingh, Die Transvaler*).

Southern Universities – MacDonald, try.
Teams:
SOUTHERN UNIVERSITIES: J. Brink; A. Read, P. Whipp, P. Goosen, L. Oosthuizen; D. Snyman, C. Wait; R. Bryant, P. Ingerson, D. Claxton, H. Muller, F. Burger, J. Coetzee, D. MacDonald, M. du Plessis (capt.).
BRITISH ISLES: A. R. Irvine; T. O. Grace, R. T. G. Bergiers, G. W. Evans, C. Rees; P. Bennett, J. Moloney; J. McLauchlan (capt.), K. Kennedy, S. Carmichael, C. Ralston, G. L. Brown, T. David, R. M. Uttley, A. Neary.
Referee: Dr J. Moolman (Eastern Province)

From the first whistle of a not-too-efficient referee, despite his training in Wales, the two sides were called 'Sealions' and 'Aqua-students' by the more imaginative members of the press box. It was splash, splash, kick and rush, and reminded me of Cardiff Arms Park in the good old days when the grass was sparse and the water and mud plentiful, but those are far off days now and the present Welsh players do not remember them, although for Gareth Edwards there was a memory of the 1970 Springbok-Wales match when he slithered over in the mud for the equalising try. For those former Springboks like John Gainsford, Dave Stewart and company it was Cardiff 1960, and for the legendary Boy Louw it was Swansea 1931. How muddy were the relationships between South Africa and Wales and here we were again, bogged down, and the first charge came from flanker Tom David, who was to enjoy an excellent match.

The Lions took the lead after seven minutes when Neary stood off a set scrum inside the students '25' and took Moloney's pass before feeding him again on the outside and the young Irish businessman sailed through the gap like a Dublin taxi to hand on to Roy Bergiers who glided over for a fine try which Andy Irvine, who was to play extremely well, converted. However it was 24 minutes into the first half before the students got their only score, a try by Dougal MacDonald, a short but clever number eight, who was fed at the back of a maul from a catch after a Lions drop out. He broke to the open side and for once the last Lions forward, whose job it was to guard the open side, was missing and MacDonald raced away to the line where he was tackled but got over for his try. The kick by Snyman failed but this score challenged the Lions.

Five minutes later Irvine kicked a superb 40 yard penalty out of the mud to be followed by another clever short line try by Gordon Brown. He jumped high to gather a throw in at a line-out outside the Universities line and crashed over in one action and although Irvine did not convert this, he kicked another penalty before the interval from 30 yards to make it 16–4 to the tourists, and they were heading comfortably for victory. During the break the Newlands Ground looked like a paddy field and one official commented . . . 'We'll never play on here again!' It was rather a pity but in all its history, it could never have looked as bad as this and must have raised the question, 'Should not the Western Province have another ground, so that this one could be rested and nutured back to health?

For over 30 minutes, the second half was splash and counter splash with occasional attempts at back play by the students, but in the main, the drive and control of the Lions forwards. However, there followed a long stream of penalties against the Lions from Referee Moolman, with ten for the Students and one of the Lions in the first half hour period. Then came a good try from the Lions when Moloney fed Bennett from a scrum moving right and he handed on to Bergiers before Irvine joined the line, ran on, and then chipped a short punt to the Students' line where Brink could not gather, and Uttley picked up and dived over for a try. Bennett could not convert but the Lions were right on top now.

In the closing minute of play, they got one more try and a good one, symbolic of their forward power. It started about ten yards out and the Lions won the strike and then 'walked' the ball and the students (slowly and surely) back to the goal line and over it, and then fell to secure a pushover try. At the time it was credited to Ken Kennedy but Gordon Brown claims it was he who touched the ball first and that it would have been behind hooker Kennedy! A good point, and so Brown gets the try in the records as one cannot award half a try to each. The whistle that ended the match brought relief to all and the second half penalty count was 15–1 in favour of the students and, even if he was put on the panel, it appeared unlikely that Dr Moolman would get a test.

South Africans at the after match reception were full of praise for the Lions although some critics argued that they could have run the ball more. I wonder. They collected four tries; gave an impressive display at forward and maintained their unbeaten record of nine wins in nine matches. It was the best start by any Lions side during the century and most satisfying, and the whole party set off on the Wednesday morning, in the rain, for the high-veld and Johannesburg. Yet they were sad at leaving the gentle Cape and, especially, the Arthurs Seat Hotel, which had cared for them so well and proved the ideal place for the comfortable housing of a touring side. The Lions will remember the good food and friendly service for many years to come. Harder things were ahead of the Lions as the flu 'bug' had struck in Cape Town It was called 'Kiwi' flu and most of us were to get it as it spread round the touring party, caught in a cold snap in Johannesburg after the mighty rains of the Cape.

CHAPTER SIX

The Second Test

When the party settled in at the tall modern hotel called the President in the centre of the cold gold city of Johannesburg, the flu bug really went to work and soon had half the party in its grip. The contrast in weather from the Cape to the Rand was considerable and the hotel, though ideally suitable for the modern jet travelling businessman, was hardly the best place for a small rugby party of sixty that was a community, living very much together. The hotel supplied what it claimed to do, and was expensive and modern, but never a rugby man's hotel.

The rooms were comfortable, but there were only ten rooms per floor and 25 floors, so all communication was by telephone as the lifts were overworked, and the Lions were never happy there, although this was due as much to the shape of the building as anything else. On arrival, and after an X-ray examination, it was discovered that Clive Rees had broken a finger and had to have his right hand put into plaster, with a probable absence of two weeks, while Doctor Ken Kennedy did a noble job with his newly acquired 'black bag'. He had to call upon myself, as I was 'laid low' with a day in bed on the Friday, and he told me that he was treating at least ten players, seven of whom were room patients. Even Manager Thomas and Coach Millar were victims, while McBride has a poisoned toe and so the selected team was full of doubtful starters on the Friday.

Transvaal officials, although concerned at the flu epidemic, must have believed their strong side, including twelve players from the champion Diggers Club, had more than a chance of lowering the Lions colours at Ellis Park on the Staturday. Messrs Jannie Le Roux, Corrie Bornmann and the 'Glass House' officials, popularly known as the 'Mafia' in South African rugby circles, welcomed the Lions at Ellis Park and the team trained on Thursday and Friday in extremely cold conditions. Vivian and myself entertained Malise Mackeurton at the President and talked of the 'Wreckers and Burners' of 1968, and those well known travelling entertainers, the 'Fizzers', three of whom were on tour again, much older and certainly less active and more staid, but with no 'Group' to challenge them!

Some Transvaal officials who had watched the First Test in Cape Town, when the Transvaal Union hired the 'Blue Train' for the round trip, were reported to hold a gloomy view of affairs, as far as the beating of the Lions was concerned during the tour, unless the Transvaal could defeat them. The control of the Lions on the softer grounds of the Cape had impressed the men of the Transvaal but they felt that their provincial side would give the Lions the hardest match of the tour to date. They could field a big pack of forwards, clever halves and strong three-quarters, and a kicking, match winning outside-half in Gerald Bosch. The Transvaal claimed that he was more than the answer to Dawie Snyman of Western Province, as kicking was more important than running!

Bosch had to play well to replace Synman in the test XV but the Transvaal, with a heavier pack, felt they could contain the Lions in front and give Bosch enough chances to kick his side to victory. The plan had not worked at Newlands against Western Province, and the rivalry between these two provinces is as keen as that between Newport and Cardiff or Llanelli and Swansea, or even Coventry and Northampton or Hawick and West of Scotland. They do not exactly love each other and consequently the 1st Test failure brought fresh criticism of Western Province and their test players.

The Friday evening before the match saw me working in bed and telephoning Cardiff with my copy, while three key players, J. P. R. Williams, Bobby Windsor and Phil Bennett, were doubtful starters, but several players got out of bed on Saturday morning, not really fit to play but, as Doctor Kennedy fell victim to the epidemic, the chosen fifteen players decided to go through with it and justify the maxim of Willie John McBride... 'There is no escape!' Several colleagues called upon me during Friday and never having missed a match, I clambered out of bed on Saturday morning, wrapped up well, and went to Ellis Park on the Press Bus, more than a little concerned at the outcome of the match, as the Lions had to contend with a big and determined Transvaal side, the altitude and flu epidemic. If they could defeat all three at the same time, and win the match, it would prove no mean achievement. Indeed, it would be the best victory of the tour, of the ten matches played up to that time, and there was many an anxious moment before victory was achieved.

Match No. 10, at Ellis Park, Johannesburg. June 15, 1974.
British Isles defeated the Transvaal by one goal, three penalties and two tries (23) to three penalties and two dropped goals (15).
Crowd: 68,000. *Weather:* Sunny. *Ground:* Firm and dry.
Scorers:
Transvaal – Gerald Bosch three penalties and two dropped goals.
British Isles – R. Milliken, J. P. R. Williams and A. Neary tries. P. Bennett three pens, one con.
Teams:
TRANSVAAL: J. Coetzer; G. Muller, P. Cronje, T. Symons, J. van der Wyngaardt; G. Bosch, P. Bayvel; T. Sauermann, D. Fredrickson, J. Strauss, J. Kritzinger, S. du Rand, C. Pypers, A. Oberholzer (capt.), K. de Klerk.
BRITISH ISLES: J. P. R. Williams; T. O. Grace, R. A. Milliken, R. T. G. Bergiers, J. J. Williams; P. Bennett, J. J. Moloney; J. McLauchlan, R. W. Windsor, F. E. Cotton, W. J. McBride (capt.), G. L. Brown, R. J. Uttley, A. Ripley, A. Neary.
Referee: Mr. P. Robbertze (Northern Transvaal).

The Transvaal began with great fire in pursuit of man and ball and after Bosch had misfired badly with his first shot at penalty goal, he put an easy one over from 20 yards to give his side an early and valuable lead. Bennett then had a kick at penalty goal from 50 yards and it sailed just wide, and he was then wide with another attempt from 30 yards to suggest that it would be Bosch's day and not Bennett's as the Transvaal side hammered away with Bosch kicking continually for position.

Bosch kicked wide with a dropped goal attempt after receiving from a line-out and the Lions had difficulty covering the ball but just got to it in time when the attackers looked like getting a try. So far it had been mostly Transvaal with an occasional Lions counter as they pushed in the set scrums and contested the line-out, and when Bosch kicked his second penalty after 28 minutes as the Lions were caught standing up at a line-out, the crowd showed its obvious and understandable delight. Here were the giant killers, the young men from the Diggers Club, the tamers of the Lions, and one had thoughts of possible defeat but, knowing how strongly the Lions finished in each previous match one expected better things to come. Five minutes later Bennett kicked the first of his three penalties when the Transvaal were trapped inside the ten yards line at the line-out. Soon afterwards Bosch kicked his third goal, a beauty from 43 yards following offside play at a maul, and it was 9–3.

Grace had a long range, running kick at penalty goal from two yards inside his own half, and one thought this but a matter of variation, although it was not a bad effort and then the interval arrived with the Transvaal comfortably placed, or so they thought, as the Lions battled against the three adversaries. Obviously, the flu and the altitude had taken their toll as J. P. R. Williams and Bobby Windsor were quite ill for a time before recovering to help in one of the most impressive fight backs of the tour.

Within two minutes of the restart the Lions went away in the loose and Windsor charged. He was held but fed from the maul for Moloney to send Milliken away. The Irish centre cleverly dummied and moved inside to cross for a much needed try, and when Bennett kicked the goal the Lions were level at 9–9. It was a vital score, and coming so quickly after the interval it put the Lions right back into the match and almost immediately they were away again in full cry, J. J. Williams being held just outside the Transvaal corner flag. It was exciting stuff which the crowd appreciated, although like a herd of Game in the bush they scented danger from this special pride of Lions. There was danger, too, although it was the Transvaal who scored next and again the three points came from the boot of Bosch. A tight head scrum was won 30 yards out and he dropped a neat right footed goal to regain the lead for his side before the Lions achieved the decisive score of the match, and the lead for the second time, which they were not to lose.

They forced a five yard scrum and Ripley picked up the ball to charge for the line and produce a try, technically, but Referee Robbertze, unsighted on the other side of Ripley, ruled another five yard scrum. The Lions won the ball again and Moloney fed Bennett who ran right and worked the scissors with Milliken for the centre to run and jink to the left, right across the defence, before finding the ever-ready J. P. R. Williams steaming up the left-wing, like a good attacking full-back, to take a long pass from Milliken and dash over for an invaluable try.

Bennett missed the conversion although it was not a difficult one for him and then made amends two minutes later with a beautifully judged penalty goal from 30 yards, after 'pulling down' at a line-out. Now it was 16–12 to the Lions, with 15 minutes to go, and one sensed that the situation would produce a 'cliff hanging' finish, and it did!

The Lions forwards were now a shade in front and getting their second wind after feeling their lungs were about to burst, while the backs recovered their running legs that had felt so leaden with tiredness. Transvaal made one final effort and took up position 30 yards from the Lions line where they won a maul and Bayvel sent it back quickly to Bosch who dropped another fine goal from 30 yards, and it was just 16–15 to the Lions. The next side to score would win the match and with a final surge as full time drew near, the Lions laid seige to the Transvaal line, as the tired provincial players held on grimly.

They cleared only to be penalised at a maul in the fortieth minute and Bennett kicked a superb goal from 45 yards. Yet another score was to come, as Moloney broke to feed Ripley, who charged before sending Neary dashing for the line and the third Lions' try. Despite the fact that Bennett was wide with the conversion, this was the decisive score, in the third minute of injury time. The Lions had achieved their finest victory of the tour to date and resisted a very real challenge from one of the stronger provinces. The Transvaal had started with confidence and enjoyed an excellent first half but the Lions had fought back with character, guts and team work, to preserve their unbeaten record and end the match as worthy winners.

It was a moment of considerable satisfaction because the Lions had produced a team effort in which the backs, and especially Milliken, J. P. R. Williams and Bennett, had figured prominently. They had scored three tries to nil. The forwards had outlasted the Transvaal pack on the highveld; an important pointer for the future and especially the Second Test and the flu and the altitude had been beaten. At the after-match reception in the Glasshouse, the two captains spoke admirably, and McBride thanked those Lions who had got out of their sick beds to play. It was the spirit of the 1974 Lions, added to their considerable skills, that carried a day that was one to remember, since everyone likes to see a competitor get up off the floor and win, and that is what these Lions did on their first visit to Ellis Park.

On Sunday morning the Lions party set of early for Rhodesia and few were concerned at the fact that the visit had been denounced by the Prime Minister as an 'outrage', since they were young sportsmen keen to play rugby and nothing else, and eager to maintain contact with rugby men all over the world. They flew in a Viscount plane to Victoria Falls and before landing circled one of the greatest natural wonders of the world, without infringing the borders of Zambia. One or two Lions did not enjoy the pilot's flying to provide a better view of the Falls, but most of them took a series of pictures of the 'Smoke that thunders'.

After landing the party moved down to the Zambezi River and boarded a launch for a trip up the river and a barbecue lunch that was thoroughly enjoyed by everyone. Giant plates of steak, salad and vegetables disappeared at an alarming rate with gallons of orange juice, milk and beer. Then a visit to a small island to chat to the friendly monkeys and back down-river to the landing stage before moving on to visit the Crocodile Farm where Bobby Windsor thought the largest 'crocs' would fit into the Pontypool pack and where Mervyn Davies was 'nipped' on the hand by a baby croc. A most unusual farm, and the 'feeding time' interlude proved how unfriendly these reptiles are when raw flesh is near at hand, be it animal or human! Ned van Esbeck was not at all impressed with the crocs and disliked them as much as he does snakes and said, 'We'd have none o' them in dear old Ireland!'

On from the Farm to the Falls, and to Livingstone's statue where Gordon Brown posed along side the famous missionary claiming he was a decendent of the great man. Broon of Troon was serious, of course, and his status in the party grew as they battled with the spray to take colour pictures of the 'Devil's Cataract'. Then through the rain forest and back to the car park short of the Border Post and on to the coach again. In happier days the party could have crossed the famous road-rail bridge and seen the 'Boiling Pot', but now there was a border indicating that the world's most intelligent animal, man, continued to cut himself off from his brother, in tribal fashion, the world over. How sad!

Then away in another Viscount to Salisbury where a warm welcome awaited with the Welsh Society holding their banners on high. Meikles Hotel in Salisbury was as warm and as grand as ever, and delighted to see us, while the Rhodesian Rugby Union gave its traditional happy reception to the Lions in the Livingstone Room . . . a perfect end to a perfect day on tour.

In all my travels round the world in search of rugby football I have felt, always, that living in Meikles is like going back to the happy 1930s as it is so essentially British; at least British in the sense that one has lived through the past fifty years, and the better traditions of living are enjoyed at this hotel. Again, there are so many rugby men there that are dear friends, Air Vice Marshall Harold Hawkins, Ken Wood, Reg Stewart, John Gibson, Bob Smith, Bob Prentice, Ian Berry and those delightful 'twins', Fred Dawe and George Pitt. Rebels in the eyes of the British Government, perhaps, but rugby men and citizens I will respect always.

I learned much from them and Cabinet minister Lardner Burke, and I sensed a much happier relationship between black and white in Rhodesia than most other countries in Africa. Yet I sensed they were concerned about the northern frontier and most of them wanted a settlement with Britain. Indeed, they need Britain as much as Britain needs them, and to see foreign cars in the streets instead of British cars as well as consumer goods from other countries in the shops, made one realise what a political and human tragedy it all is, as the Rhodesians are more British than the British at the moment.

Before the match, the Goshawks Club held a special lunch with Ken Wood in the chair and Harold Hawkins present as founder and president, while Vivian and myself were the chief guests and invited to speak. We attempted to thank them and tell them that we really wanted to visit them and see the Lions play against Rhodesia, and that we did not think they were 'rebels'.

Match No. 11, at Police Ground, Salisbury. June 18, 1974.
British Isles defeated Rhodesia by three goals, three penalties, three tries and one dropped goal (42) to two penalties (6).
Crowd: 22,000. *Weather:* Sunny. *Ground:* Firm and dry.
Scorers:
Rhodesia – I. Robertson two penalties.
British Isles – Steele, Grace(2), Edwards, Slattery, Irvine tries.

Irvine three cons, three pens, one dropped goal.
Teams:
RHODESIA: I. Robertson; E. Barrett, P. Semple, L. Lloyd-Evans, J. Harris; I. Lendrum, D. Christian (capt.); A. Van Zyl, T. Chamney, R. Coleshaw, G. Hodgson, M. Jakobi, P. Chalmers, B. Murphy, R. Woodman.
BRITISH ISLES: A. R. Irvine; T. O. Grace, R. T. G. Bergiers, G. W. Evans, W. C. C. Steele; I. R. McGeechan, G. O. Edwards (capt.); A. B. Carmichael, K. W. Kennedy, F. E. Cotton, R. M. Uttley, C. W. Ralston, S. A. McKinney, T. M. Davies, J. F. Slattery.
Referee: Mr S. Strydom (Orange Free State).

The Lions received a warm reception on taking the field and played the first half with the strong sun at their backs, prepared to face it in the second half with an anticipated long shadow down the field. They were soon in the lead when Andy Irvine kicked his first penalty and then gathered 30 yards out and dropped a smart goal to suggest that a big score was on the way, as indeed it was, but not at first, as Rhodesia battled bravely, indicating their desire to keep play fluid and not tangle too closely with the big Lions pack that contained four test men.

The promising and skilful Rhodesian full-back, Ian Robertson, proved to be a splendid orthodox 'straight through' place-kicker, as well as a fine catcher of the ball and long range touch finder. He brought Rhodesia level with two excellent penalty goals after 16 minutes play, and the crowd were delighted before the more experienced Lions pulled away and Steele got a try, followed by one from Grace that Irvine converted. Near the interval, the brilliant Edwards moved sharply to the blindside and raced 60 yards with the speed of a wing to end up behind the posts for a superb try which Irvine converted. While Edwards was running in for the try, two players were 'wrestling', Andre Van Zyl, the Rhodesian prop, and Mervyn Davies. When the 'bout' ended, Davies showed his arm to Doctor Kennedy and one suspected a possible 'bite' but no one complained afterwards. As the Rhodesians said, there was no shortage of meat in their country, and I had to agree, for the steaks were superb, especially when Fred and George entertained!

Thus at half time it was 25 points to six in favour of the Lions, as Irvine heralded an outstanding second half as an attacking full-back by kicking his second penalty goal before the interval whistle to make his tally 13 points at that stage. In the second half he collected a try, a penalty and converted his try, which was a beauty, while Grace and Slattery also got tries. Slattery's was due to a quick charge down of a clearing kick that rebounded, and he was over the line to touch down before one could say 'Rhodesia'.

Irvine fielded a clearing kick five minutes from the end of the match 30 yards out and swerved and dodged past four defenders before touching down and the crowd rose to him. It was his day, and the members of the Press Box, including myself, put his name forward as a candidate for strong consideration for a test place. The match ended with the Lions winning 42 points to six but it was a thoroughly entertaining game, made more so by Rhodesia's willingness to move their limited supply of possession. They realised beforehand that they could not beat the mighty Lions so they devoted their efforts to sharing in the attractiveness of the play, and deserve credit for their approach.

At the after-match function, Premier Ian Smith stood in the crowd and listened to the speeches and was then introduced to the Lions' management, captain and leading players, chatting to McBride and Edwards, who had met him previously in 1968. I had a short chat with him and found that he had aged considerably through worry and heavy responsibility but we did not know at the time the he was to dissolve the Rhodesian Parliament on the next day, in his bid to achieve unity in his own land, before making yet another attempt to achieve a settlement with Britain. May the day not be too far away because there is hope for black and white living together, happily, in the lovely land.

With only two direct lines from Salisbury to London, the local post office did a good job of work in getting the copy out while the *Rhodesian Herald*'s editor and staff were most helpful to the visiting press. The evening's celebrations were pleasant and then it was away to Pretoria in the morning on the SAA 747 after many fond farewells, as everyone in the party had thoroughly enjoyed the 'illegal' visit as rugby men. On the giant plane one used the headphones to listen to selections from 'Cabaret' and 'Gigi' while partaking of lunch. Air travel gets better every day but what will happen when the Concorde streaks through the sky? Can they grow much bigger and travel become much faster?

The 747 is big enough for me, but then, so much has happened in 50 years, and from Col. Lindbergh to the 747 is a giant step as mechanical progress cannot be denied even if the world's postal services grow slower and slower. One thinks of many things when 30,000 feet up in the air, and this is good for the soul!

The Lions were ready for duty on arrival at the Union Hotel in Pretoria and immediately set off for a training session at which coach Millar gave no indication whether any changes would be made in the test team. On Thursday morning Thomas and Millar announced the side as unchanged, which was the correct thing to do, as the team had won the test at Cape Town decisively and was well worthy of a chance to prove its quality while playing on the highveld. It had spirit, character, guts and skill, and it wanted to succeed on the highveld in a test match after playing so well against the Transvaal and Rhodesia. When the name of the referee was announced as Cas de Bruyn, one realised how much thought the management and captain had given to the matter, which was of vital importance to the conduct of the match.

Mr de Bruyn had not enjoyed a happy match at Windhoek and had apologised to Syd Millar, privately, on this point and thus it was thought he would be determined to be at his best, if he were awarded a test match. The psychological approach appeared sound enough and when it was all over, neither side could have any complaint against Mr de Bruyn in a match that was clean, wholesome and played in the best of spirit. What panel would be presented for the Third Test was a matter of conjecture although the Lions did not expect Max Baise to be on it. The agreement was that the SA Board would nominate four referees for each test, from which the Lions management could select and if they required a man outside the panel they could nominate a fifth but, he would have to receive the approval of the SA Board. Then, if the Board should chose to reject the fifth referee, they would then nominate a sixth who would be in charge of the match.

This happened for the Second Test of 1968, and because the SA Board would not agree to the fifth man, it appointed a sixth, much to the annoyance of David Brooks, the Lions manager, and it was from that moment that the tour went slightly astray and, unfortunately, a gap divided David Brooks and Danie Craven for the rest of it. After the Second Test the 1968 Lions realised that they would be forced to have only those referees the SA Board approved, and Syd Millar and I discussed this at length in Pretoria, while thinking of ways in which to have the referees the Lions thought to be the best, as most rugby men appreciate the value of a referee who is consistent and who watches both sides and, up to this stage of the tour, Max Baise and Cas de Bruyn had done their best in the Tests and earned no complaint from either side, despite the fact that South African officials and press had criticised the Lions line-out play earlier in the tour.

The Springboks gathered together on the Wednesday at their hotel like knights on a crusade, determined at all costs to level the series, and coach Johaan Classen ordered a 'security' clamp-down. His team and reserves went to the Pretoria Prison Ground to train, so they would not be observed by outsiders, and he banned his party from reading newspapers as it was thought these would disturb the younger players. The tension mounted for them and, while appreciating to the full the task that confronted them and that they had to overcome the handicap of not having played Tests for two years, one did feel they were taking the situation far too seriously.

In contrast the Lions had another public practice on Thursday at which Fran Cotton and Sandy Carmichael were engaged in a temporary 'brush' in the front row and this small 'incident' made banner headlines across the top of the front page of one of the Afrikaans language morning papers! On Friday the Lions relaxed at the Union Hotel as it filled up with supporters, while the Springboks set off with their training kit in a coach for an unknown destination. The British Press tried to get calls in and out of the hotel but the small switchboard, large enough for normal purposes was overwhelmed by the demands, without any great success. Fortunately, the *Mail and Echo* switchboard got me each day with only five minutes delay; so I had no complaint and on Sunday morning I got through to Cardiff to speak to my wife and son without any delay.

By Friday evening the hotel had become a Persian Market as supporters searched for tickets and then haggled over prices, to remind me strongly of Friday evenings in Cardiff before a big international match. It was reported that tickets were fetching ten times their face value since the whole of South Africa appeared to regard the Second Test as the 'big' one, while the efficient secretary, Robert Denton and his North Transvaal RU staff were extremely busy making the final match arrangements at the giant Loftus Versveld Ground in the residential area of Arcadia. A tall, handsome young man in his early 30s, who played at lock for Northern Transvaal and graduated at the local university, Robert Denton possessed considerable charm and efficiency, and while chatting in his office, Vivian and myself learned much about the big business of South African rugby, and that the takings in ticket money for the test would be over R300,000, which was nearly £200,000, a much larger figure than that for any of the home internationals in the British Isles. Little wonder the Northern Transvaal Union were well on their way to completing what will be the best test arena in South Africa.

On Friday I lunched with the Editorial staff of the new 'Rugby' magazine run by the Northern Transvaal Union, at least two of its members in Mrs Joan Swiegers, wife of Professor Daan Swiegers the Springbok selector, and Quintus van Rooyen, the Sports Editor of the sunday paper, *Rapport*. Joan was extremely enthusiastic about the game and the magazine, believing in the maxim where father and sons are rugby men that if you 'cannot beat them, join them'. Mike Gibson arrived from home looking lean and fit and, as always, a little pale, but full of enthusiasm while Alan Old rejoined the party from Cape Town on his crutches. He looked well on arrival but was prevented from watching the match through gastroenteritis, although he went off with the party to the Game Reserve on Sunday. Alan told me that he would continue playing next season to get match fit in order that he would be able to coach the game at school, while he hoped to play a great deal of Minor Counties cricket for Durham.

Saturday morning arrived with hundreds outside the hotel on the lawns drinking merrily, discussing the match as well as hoping to catch a glimpse of the Lions. It was test match fever of epidemic proportions and Pretoria was alive with noisy supporters, much as Cardiff is on an international match Saturday morning. A picnic lunch at the ground with Mal and his group brought back the memories of sad matches when defeat stared the Lions in the face, even before the kick off! Now it was all so different, and the Lions were taking the field to win. How warm the sun seemed; how gay the atmosphere at Loftus Versveld; how confident we all were in those hours of waiting!

There was a bubbling excitement in the crowded stands and the Lions emerged from the dressing-room tunnel to check on the ground and atmosphere, and they appeared casual and relaxed, as if it was just another match, signing autographs and chatting away gaily. Phil Bennett emerged and absorbed the atmosphere before hurrying back as he removed his tie. I wonder if he thought then that it was to be 'his' afternoon, in the sense that he was to be the star of the show, and that in brilliant company. Back in the dressing-room it was the captain, who uttered the last words of motivation, and McBride said, 'This is the most important match of my life. It is the most important match of the tour. We must win it!' These words were enough; the fuse was lit, and the Lions cannonade would be powerful and successful. At that moment the team was prepared to die for its captain. That was the spirit of the 1974 Lions.

Match No. 12. The Second Test at Loftus Versveld, Pretoria. June 11, 1974.
British Isles defeated South Africa by one goal, one dropped goal, one penalty, and four tries (28) to one dropped goal and two penalties (9).
Crowd: 63,000. *Weather:* Warm and sunny. *Ground:* Firm and dry.
Scorers:
South Africa – G. Bosch one dropped goal and two penalties.
British Isles – J. J. Williams(2), P. Bennett, G. L. Brown, R. A. Milliken tries. P. Bennett one conversion, one penalty. I. R. McGeechan one dropped goal.
Teams:
SOUTH AFRICA: I. McCallum (WP); G. Germishuys (OFS), P. Whipp (WP), J. Snyman (OFS), C. Pope (WP); G. Bosch (Tvl), P. Bayvel (Tvl); N. Bezuidenhout (NT), D. Fredrickson (Tvl), J. H. F. Marais (EP) (capt.), J. Williams (NT), K. de Klerk (Tvl), J. Ellis (SWA), M. de Plessis (WP), D. MacDonald (WP). Replacement: D. Snyman (WP) for McCallum and L. Vogel (OFS) for Snyman.
BRITISH ISLES: J. P. R. Williams (W); W. C. C. Steele (S), R. Milliken (I), I. R. McGeechan (S), J. J. Williams (W); P. Bennett (W), G. O. Edwards (W); J. McLauchlan (S), R.

Windsor (W), F. E. Cotton (E), W. J. McBride (I) (capt.), G. L. Brown (S), R. M. Uttley (E), T. M. Davies (W), J. F. Slattery (I).
Referee: Mr C. de Bruyn (Transvaal).

When the teams emerged from the darkness of the dressing-room tunnel into the sunlight, there were loud cheers from an expectant crowd and it was Bennett who set the match in motion with the sun behind him, and Edwards kicked from the first scrum to the corner before the Lions were penalised at the first line-out. Steele was rather nervous dealing with a Springboks rush up the left touch line and, suddenly, I realised how great was the tension in these opening minutes. Then Bosch had a glorious chance to launch a score which a more experience player would have accepted for he moved away on a Bayvel pass and turned inside Slattery, who had fanned out to cover any attempt by Bosch to drop a right footed goal, and since Bosch spotted the speeding Slattery early enough, he jinked inside and then with de Plessis moving up on his left side, ready for the vital pass, Bosch kicked on to J. P. R. Williams and the full-back cleared. Yet the move had threatened at first, and for ten minutes the Springboks played with considerable spirit.

Bennett kicked wide after 11 minutes with a 25 yards penalty attempt which normally he would have chipped over, before the first score of the match was produced by two enthusiastic Welshmen. Edwards kicked into the 'box' from a 30 yards scrum with just enough height and distance, perfectly judged, for John J. Williams to run on to the dropping ball and fly kick it to the Springbok line. The defence fell behind him as he raced on to touch down and score a clever try, typical of the alert approach of the Lions, not only in creating opportunities but executing and accepting them. Once again Bennett was wide, as he was with a penalty attempt soon afterwards.

Then McCallum attempted a penalty shot from 48 yards and Bosch kicked wide from 30 yards. It was not a day for kickers although conditions were perfect, and the 'boy with the bucket and tee earth' readily available. After thirty minutes the Lions scored again, and I feel this was one of two decisive scores in the match. Bennett started running from his own line, *al la* Barbarians match at Cardiff 1972, in a wide arc to his right from near his own goal line. McBride was with him, handling perfectly, and Milliken, then McBride again, and on to Uttley, who just could not gather and appeared to knock forward slightly but Edwards drove the ball on, upfield, away from the right touch before John J. Williams came steaming across from the left wing to gather the bouncing ball 20 yards out and race over. Bennett converted this one and the Lions were ten points ahead.

Shortly afterwards, Bennett, now brimful of confidence, pace and sparkle, worked a clever switch with Milliken, moving left, and John J. Williams was put in possession only to be tackled into the corner flag by a desperate covering defender. Bosch at the other end of the field received from Bayvel, moving right, and dropped a smooth 30 yards goal to make it 10 points to three at the interval with the Lions looking good, and although they were not yet dominating, one sensed their growing power. The backs were moving so well and smoothly with Edwards, Bennett, Milliken and Williams constantly threatening and Bennett looking the complete pivot although missing, what were for him, several reasonable kicks at goal. McBride and Marais gathered their men about themselves during the interval for serious 'pep' talks but one felt it was to be the 'day of the Lion', or the 'Gry-Lion' as Wilbur Smith calls it, unless the Springboks could hit back immediately the second half started.

It was a vigorous resumption and after two minutes the Springboks had reduced the lead when a penalty was awarded on the Lions '25' and Bosch made no mistake with his high kick between the posts. They were back in the match again, and when Bosch kicked wide with a high drop at goal from 40 yards one appreciated that the challenge was on and the Lions would have to raise their game even higher to lay the bogy of Loftus Versveld, which had remained active since 'General' Morgan and his men won there in 1955, and it was another outside-half that killed the spell with a superb try.

The active Slattery gathered from a maul near mid-field and set off round the back of it into the open with Bennett on his outside and, like a good flank forward, handed on the ball some 48 yards from the Springboks line and away went Bennett on a bewildering run that left defenders non-plussed. His last jink left Ian McCallum at full-back and Bennett was over for a magnificent try that was roundly applauded by the crowd although they must have realised then that it was the second decisive one of the match.

As Bennett walked back, he started to limp and looking down at his right boot he saw blood pouring from his instep and he stopped before reaching the conversion point to call for attention. His ankle had been grazed by McCallum's boot and the studs cut his instep, but he refused to leave the field to have stitches inserted. Nothing would persuade him to leave, and after the match five stitches were necessary but he continued limping and darting in turn although still effective. Edward's attempt at the conversion sailed wide but six minutes later another try came.

Bennett harrassed Bosch in defence inside the Springboks '25' and he handed on to McCallum who was also forced to kick in a hurry. The ball did not reach touch but fell into the ready arms of the waiting Edwards who moves, invariably, on the these occasions towards the touch line in anticipation of the short falling ball. He shot straight up field like a miniature tank and, when challenged, he had the big Scottish lock, Broon of Troon, inside him. Edwards sent the ball inside at the right moment and, as Gordon Brown said, 'Nothing was going to stop me then – there was no escape for the defence!' Over he went for the try and the Lions were 18–6 in the lead despite the fact that the injured Bennett with his painful instep was just wide with the conversion attempt. This was fine rugby with the Lions attacking continually to turn the screw tighter and tighter, from which there was, as McBride said afterwards, 'no escape!' It was the day of the Gry-Lion.

After 23 minutes, a flicker of hope was raised for South Africa and, momentarily, the crowd had something to cheer, when Bosch was given another penalty attempt from 44 yards and he kicked an excellent goal to make it 18–9. Could they do more? Could Hannes Marais get something special out of his men? McCallum was rather unhappy with his right arm hanging more or less limp and, finally, one saw Marais speak to him and the full-back left for the dressing-room. On came Dawie Snyman as a replacement at full-back and, immediately, he joined an attack, moving the ball smoothly to add some rhythm to a disjointed back line.

McGeechan who had not scored any points but performed extremely well on tour up to this stage with intelligent resourceful play, decided to take a hand in the 'killing' of the Springboks, much as Jeff Butterfield had done on the same ground in 1955. The ball came back at a line-out from the Lions pack that was now going really well and Edwards sent a long flat pass at speed to Bennett standing up with rare confidence, despite his obvious limp. Bennett handed on to McGeechan, running into the pass at speed. The centre suddenly checked and dropped left footed for goal. The ball sailed high between the posts. It was a 'death blow' and one felt the hearts of the players and spectators alike sink. There was no escape now; the wheel had turned the full circle, and the Lions were rampant, racing away to a record victory.

Yet the scoring had not ended; neither had South Africa's troubles, for Dawie Snyman, on the field for less than ten minutes, suddenly fell in a tackle while on the attack and did not rise. He suffered a suspected fracture of the leg above the ankle and had to be removed on a stretcher. The second replacement full-back arrived on the field in the person of the young Free State wing Leon Vogel, and his first involvement was a late tackle high on Bennett after the outside-half had kicked. Down went Bennett and a penalty was correctly awarded where the ball landed. Bennett revived quickly and was 'determined to take the kick to show I was as tough as anybody else'. With his damaged instep, he landed the goal from 25 yards and said, 'I felt much better after that because I had missed several kickable goals, and that always annoys me.' The match entered injury time and Bosch kicked wide with a 30 yard penalty attempt before the Lions achieved their final try, the fifth of the afternoon, to complete their rout of the Springboks.

It was the 'master' again, at scrum-half, the supreme performer Edwards, who moved sharply to the blind side on the Springboks '25' line and, leaning forward, he was away, finding Dick Milliken, now a fine strong centre in his own right, up with him. The sharp pass was made and Milliken crashed through the first tackle and then charged at two defenders on the goal line. They could not stop him and he rolled over to score. Bennett did not kick the goal and the final whistle sounded at 28–9 to provide the heaviest test defeat ever suffered by the Springboks in South Africa; indeed, it was more, their heaviest defeat in test rugby.

The crowd raced on to the field and almost all congratulated the Lions but one disappointed supporter, tackled Edwards and brought him to earth, on one of the rare occasions on the tour. Hannes Marais shook the offender free and handed him to the police, and he was taken to the dressing-rooms to apologise to Edwards. End of incident!

As the well-known figures in South African rugby trooped by the Press Box they offered congratulations readily to the British Press, and so did members of the South African press, and one felt moved by it all. Twenty years had been a long wait to see British rugby at the top of the world tree again, and such a fine display of attractive, efficient, determined team work had made it all seem worthwhile for those many officials and coaches back home, in all four countries, and for Alun Thomas and his Lions party.

Again, for McBride, for Millar, for Edwards, for McLauchlan, for Mervyn Davies and those senior players who had provided the platform of experience on which this quite remarkable side was constructed. The forward play had been perfect and the back play a revelation with Bennett playing his 'dream game' to establish himself as an all round test player and clinch a place alongside those other Welsh outside halves, Cliff Morgan and Barry John, who had starred previously in dramatic test victories. Bennett had joined the elite, and the modest little man from Llanelli was a hero among heroes. For McBride it had proved the greatest day and the most important match of his life. The Lions could not now lose the series and the first part of 'Mission 1974' had been completed. McBride could take his place alongside Sidney John Dawes and bid for even greater honour. No Lions side had scored two successive victories in this century . . . no wonder we were tempted on Saturday night to call these the 'greatest'.

CHAPTER SEVEN

Thoughts on South African Rugby

It is easy to imagine the happiness in the Lions camp on the Saturday night after the Second Test as the players and camp followers celebrated quietly, wearing smiles that were broad and eyes that sparkled, for it had been a great victory. Every South African we met was full of praise. For them the disappointment was great but there were no sour grapes to spoil the occasion. Not even the referee was blamed!

The victory had put British Rugby firmly at the top of the tree and was a symbol of the reward for many years of hard work by officials at international and club level, coaches and coaching organisers, and players in all grades. The high standard of team work had been produced only by years of devotion on the part of the clubs and then the national sides and, finally, the Lions management of 1971 followed by that of 1974. At Loftus Versveld on June 22, we witnessed the finished product in action; a superb team.

There may have been many greater individual players in past Lions sides and I can think of many in the 1950s, with two great sides touring 1955 and 1959, and had either of these been subject to intensive coaching and preparation, then they would have won their respective series easily, make no mistake about this judgement. Now we are in a new era in which British forward play has reached the heights and climbed back to the high pedestal it was on before the 'take over', at the start of the present century, by the mighty touring teams from New Zealand and South Africa.

The British learn their rugby lessons the hard way and it was not so much the need of change in technique that followed the defeats of the early 1960s but the desire for fresh and enlightened thinking about the game and a new approach. There were several returning coaches who wanted change, Alun Thomas, John

Robins and Ronnie Dawson. If the Welsh were the first to launch the revolution, it took time to take effect even in radical Wales. However, once the Welsh had grasped the nettle firmly there was no stopping their improvement and the Coaching Committee, coach organiser, national selectors and team coach, were able to produce fine sides in 1969–72. The other Home Countries soon followed and by 1974 they were on a par again which appeared as a stalemate to the outside world, but which produced a high standard of forward play in the 1974 Lions.

In South Africa the picture was quite different for they were under the handicap of diminishing international competition and after the 1969–70 tour of the British Isles, where a brave well disciplined side struggled through, there must have been a feeling that unless there was some change and possibly merit selection, the Springboks would never again visit the British Isles. They were however welcomed in France in 1974. The visit to Australia in 1971, though successful, caused considerable demonstration which led to action by the new Australian government and no Springbok sides will visit there unless there is selection on merit.

The isolation and fading prowess of South African rugby was best illuminated by the success of the England side in 1972 under John Pullin. They remained unbeaten and won the test match at Ellis Park, this following after the successful Lions 1971 tour of New Zealand, suggested that while the game in the Southern Hemisphere was not as powerful as it was, British rugby, technically and in overall application, had improved. England confirmed this by defeating New Zealand in Auckland in 1973 and so it was felt that the 1974 Lions would have a reasonable chance in South Africa because of a drop in standards, the lack of a unified coaching system and a lack of international competition.

After the Second Test one believed British rugby to be superior to that of South Africa. Form and ability varied among the provinces and the Lions were to receive two very severe jolts in the week following the Second Test which were a reminder that whatever was wrong technically, there was nothing in South African rugby that could not be put right by proper application over a period. The spirit, as revealed by the Quaggas side, playing a touring team for the first time, and the Orange Free State side, was still as strong as ever.

What was needed at this stage was a unified coaching system to be employed in all provinces and a closer look at the strength of the far too numerous provincial sides. The splitting of the major rugby provinces into smaller units was, maybe, much better for administration but certainly was not necessarily for the quality of the rugby. However, it did favour what is now known as the Free State, as it now comprises eight clubs in Bloemfontein, and the Free State looked as near to a top British club as one can imagine in its team work and spirit. That is why they achieved a moral victory over the tourists.

The press were full of praise for the Lions after the Second Test although some armchair critics poured much wrath upon the losing Springboks without, perhaps, understanding to the full the problems of the selectors and players alike. The *Star* Newspaper in Johannesburg published a short leader on the point which read as follows . . .

'Forgive us if we don't call for an immediate commission of enquiry into what happened at Loftus Versveld. It was a great game with no punch-ups, and we're proud of the Springboks for their sportsmanship that makes good losers as well as winners. That's what rugby is all about, though a whole generation of South African schoolboys was in danger of forgetting it. If we do lose the world rugby crown, it's no disaster – just an exciting challenge for the next Springboks to win it back again.'

Some of the Afrikaans press did not spare their beaten heroes but it was a fine rugby match played in excellent spirit, except for Mr Vogel's flying late tackle, and on Sunday a tired but happy Lions party set off for the Kruger National Park Game Reserve in accordance with custom and tradition. Some engaged in a 'massive' and a few boisterous exploits but none were reported and all was well!

Several of the Press Party remained in Johannesburg and took up residence at the new and comfortable Landdrost Hotel in the centre of the City. The service, comfort and atmosphere proved pleasant and relaxing, and one was able to work, deal with administrative matters and meet several long-standing friends resident in the city. Vivian, Dewi and myself (what a pity Cliff was missing) paid an official call upon Little Farm where Manager Mal and Joannie staged one of their special 'bowl of soup' suppers and to the surprise of the 'Fizzers', the President of the Group was a guest to help the delightful conversation and the occasional song into the early hours of the morning. Other friends were Ralph Daniel and family, Alan Melville and Ernie Franks, not forgetting Jeppe and Olga Van Heerden who have cared for us on every visit since the War. One makes new friends along the way, but the long standing friends are those we enjoy seeing most and, as is the custom, out came the snaps to reveal the latest developments and additions to the Thomas family. Again the weather was much better on this visit to Johannesburg and lunches at the 'Kitchen' found B.T. in good form, while the Lions were particularly pleased when they returned from the Game Reserve on Wednesday afternoon to inspect the amenities of the Landdrost.

The next match on the list, against the Quaggas at Ellis Park, was the 13th of the tour and the Lions fielded only three of the successful test side plus several players returning after long breaks through injury. Mike Burton, happily, was declared fit at last, Tom David was given a run, and Mike Gibson made his first appearance of the tour, only six days after his arrival and at an altitude of almost 6,000 feet. McGeechan played at outside-half for the second time and Fran Cotton was given the captaincy for the first time. The Quaggas were formed in 1956 as a South African Barbarians, although there is a rival club with the name of Barbarians operating successfully in Natal and both clubs have done much good for the game. It was believed that the Quaggas would pick a young side with all its members new to the Lions but, instead, they selected an experienced side with some outstanding youngsters including the Western Province under-20 outside-half, Peter Kirtsen, in what was to be his first senior match and how well he acquitted himself. When the teams fielded there was a crowd of 50,000 inside Ellis Park and almost at once the match became an extra trial as the South African selectors were present.

Match No. 13, at Ellis Park, Johannesburg. June 27, 1974.
British Isles defeated the Quaggas by one goal, two penalties and two thries (20) to four penalties and one try (16).
Crowd: 51,000. *Weather:* Dry. *Ground:* Firm and Dry.
Scorers:
Quaggas – A. Stephenson try. P. Kirsten four penalties.
British Isles – A. Ripley and G. L. Brown(2) tries. A. Irvine two penalties and one con.

Teams:
QUAGGAS:
J. Coetzer; K. Thoressen, J. Cowley, P. Cronje, A. Stephenson; P. Kirsten, P. Bayvel; J. Strauss, G. Strydom, D. Van der Berg, S. du Rand, B. Kapp, P. Fourie, J. Kritzinger, C. Pypers.
BRITISH ISLES:
A. R. Irvine; C. Rees, R. T. G. Bergiers, C. H. M. Gibson, T. O. Grace; I. R. McGeechan, J. Moloney; F. E. Cotton, (capt.) K. W. Kennedy, M. A. Burton, C. W. Ralston, G. L. Brown, A. Neary, A. G. Ripley, T. P. David.
Referee: I. Gourlay (Natal).

In the first minute Irvine kicked a penalty goal from 37 yards after a Quaggas infringement at the first line-out. Peter Kirsten the 'new boy' and darling of the crowd, despite his future challenge for the local favourite, Gerald Bosch, equalised after five minutes with a penalty from 25 yards when Lions were caught standing up inside the 10 yard mark at a line-out. The Quaggas then crossed the Lions line through centre Cowley but he was recalled and Gibson made a burst to return the Lions to the attack. He kicked through a loose ball and Ripley followed suit, to chase after the ball in hot pursuit and win the race to the line for a try that Irvine converted.

There followed long periods of Quaggas pressure, and for a scratch side they were doing extremely well while the relaxed Lions appeared out of touch. Cowley failed with a penalty attempt but the Quaggas were nearly over on the left when Thoressen was stopped by a fine tackle from Irvine. However, they could not be denied, and when McGeechan's clearing kick failed to find touch, Kirsten sent his backs moving right with ease and accuracy. The ball was moved sharply, and Stephenson was left with a clear gallop for the line and a try that found the large midweek crowd ready to make whoopee in celebration! Again, the kick was given to Cowley and he failed, and one feels certain that Kirtsen would have kicked the penalty and conversion.

Back came the Lions, eager to increase their lead before the interval, but they dithered and dallied for some time before Clive Rees set along the left touch line with his forwards in support on the inside. They handled and Gordon Brown, at the end of a fine driving rush, got the try although Irvine's kick was wide and the score was 13–7 at the interval. The Lions had looked unlike their normal selves because they could not win enough possession and the backs did not possess good rhythm while Grace was unhappy on the right wing. The Quaggas were going well with a full head of high altitude steam, especially their forwards and the two halves, test scrum-half Paul Bayvel and the under-20 Peter Kirsten, who was to do even better in the second half.

The Lions obtained no early score in the second half and it was Kirsten who scored, kicking his second penalty, this time from 40 yards, and made it 13–10, but soon afterwards Irvine (the Lions owed him much on this testing day) kicked an equally good 40 yards penalty to make it 16–10. After 20 minutes Bayvel went off with hamstring trouble and was replaced by an equally enthusiastic G. Schutte from Griquas.

The Quaggas kept at it and had slightly the better of the play, with the Lions only counter attacking occasionally. Mike Gibson settled to his task and helped Irvine in defence and another wonderful tackle by the full-back, near the corner, kept out the Quaggas full-back, Coetzer, who is normally a centre. Forwards like Van der Berg, Strauss, Kapp, Fourie and Kritzinger were going well, the last named at No. 8, was as good as any one on the field.

After 34 minutes, another penalty kick was taken by Kirsten, and this time he dropped a goal from 45 yards and it was a beauty, high between the posts to make it 16–13, and again the crowd erupted in appreciation. It was a ding-dong, hard, fast struggle between David and Goliath in rugby, and the young David was doing extremely well. Then came a score that was to spark off fierce reaction when the match ended. Gibson counter attacked cleverly and made ground before the ball was moved right through Irvine, Ripley and David to reach Brown. From the Press Box there was a suggestion of a 'knock on' but the Referee was probably unsighted. When Brown charged for the line he landed on his back before turning over to score and some in the crowd may have believed that defenders hands were on the ball was well, but Brown confirmed otherwise.

The try was allowed but there was a hold-up as oranges and other missiles were thrown at the referee and place kicker Irvine from that corner of the crowd, as they did not believe a try should have been awarded! However, it was, and although there was some doubt, a South African referee had awarded the score.

The match proceeded well into injury time and in the fifth minute, Kirsten kicked his fourth penalty from 35 yards when Maloney pushed Schutte as he was in the act of playing the ball. It was now 20–16 and no more time was available. Immediately, the final whistle blew the crowd rushed on to the ground and one 'sportsman' felled the referee, to launch a free for all as players attempted to shield the referee who was on the ground.

It was the first time I had seen such a happening, and I have seen many hard matches and controversial decisions, but this had been a particularly sporting match with the Quaggas doing a great job and almost lowering the Lions colours. Blows were aimed at Mr Gourlay and he sustained a black eye before the police rushed on to the field, some with dogs, to drive the irate crowd away. He eventually got to the tunnel and was locked away by officials while the police cleared the crowd and the chief assailant.

Twelve minutes from the actual and sensational end of the match, the Welsh wing, Clive Rees was ordered from the field by the Lions' management and replaced by J.P.R. Williams who went to full-back with Andy Irvine moving to the left wing in place of Rees. The cruellest of misfortune befell Rees, a modest and excellent tourist and more than useful wing, because 'lightning did strike twice' as far as he was concerned and he suffered another kick on the finger which was mending from the original injury suffered at Cape Town, and it was refractured. He did not want to leave the field but masseur Dave Goddess on the touch was told to call him off in case of further injury.

He was x-rayed during the evening and had the fracture confirmed, his hand was put into plaster again, which was extremely unfortunate for the player and the side, but he accepted it quietly and without complaint. Immediately it was confirmed, Manager Alun Thomas spoke to Albert Agar in London and asked if Gerald Davies was available to travel as a replacement. On Friday at Bloemfontein there were several calls and late in the evening a message came stating that although at first he thought he would come, Davies later informed the Four Home Unions secretary that he was not available to travel for domestic reasons, as he was moving back to Cardiff and had to purchase a house to settle his family in before taking up a new post with the Sports Council on August 1. In his place the Home Unions invited

Alan Morley of Bristol and England, a strong powerful wing, to replace Rees. He accepted readily and agreed to fly out from England on the Monday to join the team at Kimberley. Morley had visited South Africa with England in 1972 and scored the winning try against the Springboks at Ellis Park.

Referring to the Referee incident again the crowd watched in stoney silence and the 'Britse Pers' were quite amazed and shocked by such reaction and indeed violence. Their typewriters clicked merrily preparing messages that would produce headlines in most of their papers. Later, the Referee said in an interview, 'I did not know much about it. After blowing the final whistle to a fine sporting match, suddenly, a man tackled me from behind and my face hit the ground. It was the first occasion for me to experience such a thing but I am not worried. I love refereeing, and will continue to do the best I can. The teams played hard and fair and there was some fine rugby.'

He may have made errors, but hardly intentional, and such was the fever abroad in the land to see the Lions lose their unbeaten record that spectators, obviously partisan, had been carried away by it all. One, in particular, may have been affected by stimulation but anyway it was a sad scene and one not appreciated by the Lions party and camp followers, especially Manager Thomas and Coach Millar, who had strong words to utter in private, yet it was, as they said, a matter for the local rugby union. The world has introduced violence into sport and while association football has been pestered with this type of scene, it was new to rugby football, at least at international level.

As for the match both manager and coach admitted that the Lions were fortunate and Syd Millar told me, 'We played badly but we won, and it is not a bad thing to have a jolt like that given to us by the Quaggas, who played well to bring us back to earth after a big test victory and a relaxing visit to the Game Reserve'. Millar, who was an understanding coach and a competitor at top level for many years, knew that his side had to go through the fiery furnace of experience and that on any tour there would be almost as many 'downs' as there were 'ups'. This was a 'down' and by the skin of their teeth they escaped defeat and the Lions appreciated it, but what they did not realise was that there was worse to come in the form of 'escape'. In this match Irvine's play was a vital factor but in the next match there was neither Irvine nor Bennett to keep their noses in front.

A pleasant evening at the Country Club with the Daniel Family, then the next day, Friday, saw the show 'on the road' once again and heading for Bloemfontein where a well prepared 'ambush' had been laid for the tourists, one that was to frighten the 'life' out of them!

After lunch the plane flew out of Jan Smuts Airport to Bloemfontein and touched down in glorious sunshine and clear air to receive a warm welcome from thousands of enthusiasts who had crowded the airport building balconies to see the unbeaten Lions. As the South African liaison officer Choet Visser was a Free Stater and lived at Bloemfontein, he was immensely proud of his fellow citizens for turning up in such force and providing a fleet of vintage cars to drive the visiting heroes from the airport to their hotel, a trip that was much enjoyed by all. The Press Gang followed behind in a city bus with Ned van Esbeck pulling the bell and acting as conductor.

It was not the traditional Maitland Hotel this time or the new President where Dewi Griffiths had a piano collapse under him in 1968 but the Bloemfontein Transito, a comfortable hotel, less than 100 yards from the Post Office and, for the Press Gang, nothing could be finer. The hotel management had provided a long table for my use as an 'office' and I was soon at work on previews and other items, all prepared with a note of caution, because one felt there was to be a real challenge from the 'Vrystaat'.

This was due to Nelie Smith and Sakkie Van Zyl, two of the most enthusiastic of the younger coaches in South Africa, they had done their home work and studied closely most of the Lions matches on tour and films of each of the home countries in action. In fact, their 'ambush' was perfectly prepared and even the sayings of the modern maestro, Carwyn James, had been incorporated in the Free State drill and nothing, but simply nothing, had been left to chance. They knew every move the Lions would make and how they would react in every situation.

On Friday evening the whole of the Press, Radio and TV Gang, were the guests of Choet Visser, his wife Joyce and their family, at his lovely home in a Bloemfontein suburb where an indoor 'braai' proved a considerable success. Much interest was shown in the cabinets containing rugby trophies from all over the world, and there is little doubt that the noble liaison officer is a generous rugby fanatic who is doing much good, in his own quiet way, for the game in South Africa. At all times on tour he was willing and ready to help the Press Gang, and provided admirable support for the Lions management, except, as he says,' on five occasions, the four Tests and the Free State match, as then I must shout for my own players!'

Match No. 14, at Kings Park Bloemfontein. June 30, 1974.
British Isles defeated the Orange Free State by a penalty and two tries (11) to a dropped goal and two penalties (9).
Crowd: 60,000. *Weather:* Warm and sunny. *Ground:* Hard and dry.
Scorers:
Orange Free State – J. Snyman one dropped goal and two penalties.
British Isles – T. M. Davies and J. J. Williams tries. S. McKinney one penalty.
Teams:
ORANGE FREE STATE: P. Strydom; J. S. Germishuys, J. Schlebusch, P. du Toit, B. Swartz; J. Snyman, G. Sonnekus; R. Stander, A. Bestbier, M. le Roux, S. Botha, J. de Bruyn, J. Swart (capt.), C. Grobler, H. Verster.
BRITISH ISLES: J. P. R. Williams; J. J. Williams, R. A. Milliken, G. W. Evans, W. C. C. Steele; I. R. McGeechan, G. O. Edwards; J. McLauchlan, R. W. Windsor, A. B. Carmichael, W. J. McBride (capt.), C. W. Ralston, S. A. McKinney, T. M. Davies J. F. Slattery.
Referee: Mr G. Bezuidenhout (Transvaal).

There was an intense international match atmosphere at the Stadium and one could feel it and liken it unto Stradey Park, Llanelli, while enjoying a picnic lunch behind the stand in the sunshine. It was a warm, sunny day and the crowd watched four curtain raisers before the big one, thoroughly enjoying every moment of the day's sport with growing anticipation. While watching the spectators drive up in their cars and carry their food and wine baskets to the stands, one could not help but notice how well built and proud were the ladies of the Free State and various hair styles they paraded in Ascot fashion. It was the big day of the year in the City and the crowd of 60,000 in the vast public arena, roared as the teams took the field.

The Lions set the match in motion and the first three penalties went against them with Jackie Snyman, the Free State outside-half who was to become one of his side's heroes, kicking just below the cross bar when he attempted a kick. J. P. R. Williams was well short when he attempted a 50 yards penalty. Actually, it was 26 minutes before the hard, keen stalemate was broken. The Free State had employed a variety of moves and the Lions were penalised 33 yards out. Up trotted Snyman and landed an excellent goal. The crowd jumped up, almost to a man and cheered his effort to the echo. First blood to the Free State and a deserved lead.

This goal inspired the Free Staters to try all the harder and the Lions were rocked back on their heels. When they attacked and brought J. P. R. Williams into the line, the scarlet jerseys were put to ground by a keen cover defence. No man spared himself in the Free State side for they fell at the feet of the Lions forwards in attempts to 'kill' the ball at the rucks and, occasionally, suffered injury as a result of 'bravado', much as did Glyn Davidge for Newport against the All Blacks in 1964. Near the interval there followed several fierce five-yard scrums and rucks outside the Free State line and, eventually, the Lions heeled for Mervyn Davies to pick up smartly, dash to the wide blind side and dive over without a hand being laid on him. It was a clever, quick-thinking try and although McGeechan could not convert it, the try enabled the Lions to lead at the interval, much to their relief and that of the camp followers and reserves in the stand.

Obviously, it was going to be an even harder second half and one felt that the Lions would have to dig deeply into their reserves of skill and stamina to match this well trained Free State side which has studied the Lions closely and knew how to apply pressure even if they risked everything to achieve it. Several players had to receive attention during the interval for cuts and abrasions even though it was not a dirty match. Early in the second half the Lions attempted one of their much favoured mid-field switches but it was sternly blocked, and then the Free State No. 8, Groebler, almost scored when he was brought down inches short of the Lions line. A five yard scrum followed and the Free State moved right but a pass was dropped; yet they kept attacking and after 12 minutes the ball came back to Jackie Snyman. The

The 4th test at Johannesburg, 27th July. Springbok lock John Williams wins the ball at a line-out (*Jan Nel, Rand Daily Mail*).

The 4th test. The Springbok flanker Jan Ellis (No. 6) is brought down by Roger Uttley, with Fergus Slattery (left) and Ian McLauchlan in support (*Jan Nel, Rand Daily Mail*).

'he disallowed try in
ıe last minute of the
th test. Fergus
lattery (7) is on the
round. Referee Max
aise (centre,
ackground) was
nsighted and ordered
five-yard scrum. J. J.
/illiams (13), Ian
IcGeechan (12) and
hris Ralston (5)
ppear to think that
lattery scored (*Gert
'attingh, Die
ransvaler*).

Above: Springbok captain Hannes Marais is carried from the field at the end of the 4th test (*Jan Nel, Rand Daily Mail*).

Below: Lions *v.* Cape Town University female students! A blissful Nigel Starmer-Smith, the BBC television commentator, is supported in the line-out by Tom Grace (foreground), and Roy Bergiers. The girls won handsomely! (*The Argus*).

Lions could not prevent him dropping a neat goal to put his side back in the lead.

J. P. R. Williams had a 30 yard penalty attempt that sailed wide and John J. Williams, following up, appeared to win the touch down for a try as the ball rolled over into the in-goal area. However, the Referee's attention had been drawn from the ball by J. P. R. Williams, indicating that the Free State players had attempted to charge his kick, and the Referee awarded another kick at goal ten yards on, which J. P. R. Williams also missed. Snyman was also short from 45 yards before the Lions eventually regained the lead after defending desperately for long periods. A penalty was awarded to the Lions at a line-out on the Free State '25'. The Referee spoke to the players before Stewart McKinney was called up to take the kick and he succeeded from a wide angle.

This brought unexpected relief to the Lions and a valuable one point lead but the enjoyment was short lived because four minutes later a penalty goal by Snyman from 40 yards, and it was a good one, almost lifted the grandstand roof off its moorings as the crowd cheered and screamed. This was thirteen minutes from the actual final whistle but only nine minutes from ordinary time, and the happenings in injury time were to decide the match and save the Lions' record. The Free State full-back was forced to carry over but the Referee awarded a drop out and it appeared as if, at long last, they would lose their proud record.

In the second minute of injury time the Lions, making a last defiant effort, stormed into the Free State '25' where lock Stoffell Botha was hurt and had to receive attention. Eventually, he had to be led to the touch-line and the replacement, Potgeiter, ran on to the field ready to join his beseiged side, but Referee Bezuidenhout had to tell him, prompted by Edwards, that the duty doctor had not yet agreed. So the vital scrum had to go down 15 yards from the Free State line with eight to seven forwards and a Free State put-in. McBride said as he went down, 'Now then Lions, let us show them we are men of character and a team with guts, and win this ball!'

It was a final appeal from a proud captain. The Lions produced an inspired eight-man shove without Windsor striking against the head and, although Free State won the strike, the Lions pushed over the ball to win possession. Mervyn Davies, the shrewdest of

No. 8s, picked up and fed Edwards charging to the blind side. A huge dummy and Edwards was nearly over but just two yards short. He thought quickly. A high lobbed pass to his inside and through came John J. Williams, the Welsh 'whippet', to gather and dive over. A try! The record was safe! The Lions jumped in the air with obvious relief. The sad, tired and extremely disappointed but brave Free Staters retired to their goal line, to await the place kick. McKinney failed but it did not matter as there was no time for the Free State to launch another effort. McKinney had another penalty attempt from 44 yards but kicked wide and then the final whistle was sounded. It was all over. The Lions were through and the record books said 11–9 to them and they had played 14 matches without defeat. It was near and in some ways they were fortunate because the Free State had played so well, but the lesson was obvious to all – never play any match without a specialist place kicker. He is the most important man in any team, in any grade, today!

The 'Britse Pers' breathed a huge sigh of relief and started away with our cables. Nelie Smith, the coach of the Free State, was pleased with his side's effort but he said, generously and in keeping with his attitude, 'The Lions were just the better side.' The crowd accepted defeat magnanimously and at the reception there were only congratulations and no complaints. The Free State captain, John Swart, spoke with blood running down his face from a cut while Besbier the hooker had a badly bruised and cut eye. Botha had his head bandaged and South African writers compared the Free State dressing-room with a casualty clearing station; they had given everything in pursuit of victory.

They had raised the drooping image of South African football. They had made South Africans feel good again and pointed the way towards success against the Lions. Willie John McBride spoke out well at the after match function and said that the match was better for the Lions then any team talk he could give them, and he praised the Free State for their effort which came so near to success. Manager Thomas presented liaison officer Visser and his wife, Joyce, with gifts on behalf of the party and the team sang a song in his honour. The atmosphere was excellent and the hosts generous in defeat.

After this escape there were genuine hopes of an unbeaten tour, but the Springboks selectors were there in force to study any weaknesses in the Lions and possible Free State candidates for the national XV. It was an important day. On the Sunday I enjoyed lunch with Nelie Smith, his wife and family, at a friend's farm, and it proved a delightful relaxation while I learned two important things. First, that Nelie Smith, a fine scrum-half and now a national selector, played all his senior rugby without a left knee cap. Some man of courage and determination. Secondly, that his attending the WRU coaches course at Aberystwyth helped him considerably in his plotting and planning for the match. Indeed, I felt here was the obvious man to succeed Johaan Classen as national team coach. His fellow coach, Sakkie Van Zyl, hopped about at the after match function with his foot in plaster. He had snapped his achilles tendon ten days previously, scrumming down against the Free State pack. What enthusiasm from coaches. Who said the spirit of South African rugby was dead?

On Monday we set off by coach for Kimberley and the 15th match of the tour. It would not be hard, they said, at Kimberley, but one could never be sure, another former Springbok, former outside-half Piet Visagie was coaching Griqualand West.

Kimberley is an interesting city and really one of the main reasons for the financial success of and political heat surrounding modern South Africa. The discovery of diamonds led, as much as the discovery of gold, to the differences of opinion between the British and Dutch settlers in Southern Africa, and many things arising from the 'rushes' helped produce the situation that culminated in the sad, indeed tragic, Boer War. Few who have not been to South Africa realise what that war was all about. Indeed few members of the British Government really know South Africa and its problems. One can easily pronounce judgement from afar, and there is much that is wrong but, who are we to tell another country how to solve a problem that the great Victorians thrust upon it, and in so many places. The grandeur of the British Empire was magnificent yet, when at the very height of its power, it never quite made the progress that would have ensured its future.

Many Afrikaaners are my trusted friends and they have every right to be heard but when the British Government cuts itself off from Southern Africa in principle, but not in trade, then they are less than the Victorians. I would ask all cabinet ministers to go to

Victoria Falls and stand by Livingstone's Statue and watch millions of gallons of the Zambezi River pounding over the magnificent falls and then ask themselves, 'How can we put this right?' They would not be so righteous. They would learn in the space of minutes, the mystery that is Africa and they would temper their outbursts with the realisation that trade is all important to the British Isles and indeed to all men on earth. The Victorians made it so. There is no escape. We have a duty and the cutting off of the umbilical cord is sad for we must remember those that went before us. The Lions of 1974 represented the thin red line, the thread of continuity since 1891, when many left the shores of the British Isles to seek their fame and fortune in Southern Africa.

There is much to be done but, please, study the problems first and then ask one's self, 'How can the indigenous people best be served?' Certainly, not by the outbursts of self righteous politicians. I believe that sportsmen get much nearer to the truth and the hearts of the people. The rugby community does not seek to become a part of politics but, as ambassadors, they are second to none. They see and hear and study. They represent the people and for this reason alone, the tour was a necessary and an important success.

Kimberley is a warm and friendly city with the De Beers Company acting as a foster parent to its development. On arrival the company staged the first multi-racial reception ever provided for a Lions team. Is this not progress? Much enjoyed by everyone, there were many faces that we recognised including the Griquas president Wally Hammond and former Springbok Dick Lockyear and his wife, while Piet Visagie was looking more studious than ever. The Braai was to have been held near the 'Big Hole' but the weather was chilly and, instead, it was at the De Beers Country Club.

Dewi Griffiths, Alun Williams and Nigel Starmer-Smith went round the country filming historical items such as locations where diamonds were first found, and native tribes. The magic of Southern Africa had Griffiths spellbound and the 'Big Hole' and its museum provided a vivid picture of man's search for wealth. Perhaps, it is man that remains the mystery and not Africa?

The Griquas had won the Currie Cup a few years previously but then they had Francois Roux and Piet Visagie to help them.

In 1974 they were not as strong, as the final score in the match against the Lions suggests, yet they played with spirit.

Match No. 15, at the De Beers Stadium, Kimberley. July 3, 1974.
British Isles defeated Griqualand West by nine goals, one penalty and three tries (69) to one goal, two penalties and one try (16).
Scorers:
Griqualand West – D. Wiese two tries, one conversion and one penalty. J. Van Eck one pen.
British Isles – T. O. Grace(4), W. C. C. Steele(2), J. J. Moloney, G. W. Evans, T. David, J. F. Slattery, A. G. Ripley, and K. W. Kennedy tries. A. R. Irvine eight conversions and one penalty. C. M. H. Gibson one conversion.
Teams:
GRIQUALAND WEST: J. Smith; O. Fourie, J. Lategan, J. van der Walt, D. Wiese; J. Van Eck, G. Schutte; J. Harrison, D. Slabbert, K. Mulder, J. Young, K. Esterhuizen, J. Lochner, Van As Jordaan, K. Bester.
BRITISH ISLES: A. R. Irvine; W. C. C. Steele, R. A. Milliken, G. W. Evans, T. O. Grace; C. M. H. Gibson, J. J. Moloney; A. B. Carmichael, K. W. Kennedy, M. A. Burton, C. W. Ralston, R. M. Uttley, T. David, A. G. Ripley, J. F. Slattery (capt.).
Referee: Mr C. de Bruyn (Transvaal).

It proved a most enjoyable match, full of good football, strong running and clever handling and although the Lions won by the second largest margin of the tour at 69–16, the Griquas played a big part in the approach and style of the game as they, too, were prepared to run with the ball and Willie McBride paid them quite a compliment at the after match function. What he said was true for it was a remarkably clean and sporting game with Mr de Bruyn refereeing well and allowing play to run. Only nine penalties were awarded and this is an indication of the accuracy of the play by both sides.

It was obvious after six minutes, when the Lions led by 12 points, that they would win comfortably, as of course they did, but the Griquas kept coming back at them especially in the second half and it was a race against time to see whether the Lions could pass the 60 points total of England's 1972 'White tornadoes'. They did so in the closing minutes of the match, much to the amusement of the London members of the Press Gang who had seen Alan Old kick so well in 1972. Actually, they stood to attention and saluted.

Tom Grace really came good with four tries and, as Syd Millar, said, 'He stretched his legs in this match!' so the reputation of the 'amazing' Grace was saved and he celebrated his return to form, watched fearfully by his 'coach' Ned Van Esbeck! Steele got two tries and Moloney, Evans, David, Slattery (after a 70 yard dash like a wing), Ripley (with a traditional charge) one apiece. The 'Doctor', Ken Kennedy, finished off a long movement for his first try of the tour. Andy Irvine was in fine kicking form and landed eight conversions and one penalty for 19 points to become the leading points scorer of the moment on tour, while Mike Gibson converted one to collect his first points.

It was 25–3 at the interval as outside-half Van Eck had kicked a penalty for the Griquas. In the second half the right-wing, Wiese, scored 13 points, much to the delight of the crowd. He got two tries, among the best of the tour scored against the Lions, converted one of them and kicked a penalty, which represented a good afternoon's work. The teams were loudly applauded when they left the field and I could not quite understand those South African critics who suggested that it was a disappointing crowd, as 8,000 was a good figure in midweek for Kimberley, especially for a match that was a foregone conclusion in the terms of a result. Intrepid rugby follower Len Bevan of West Wales was interviewed by Alun Williams after this match and said he did not think the 1974 Lions side was as good as that of 1971.

It was a very early start from Kimberley, and on the morning after a match rugby sides are not especially good at rising with enthusiasm and dashing to the airport. I cannot say I blame them as I am a reluctant hero also in the mornings, at least at such an hour, but in the southern hemisphere they are early risers and think nothing of it. Most of them go to bed much earlier than a Lions party on match days! Eventually, the party reached the airport rather 'bug-eyed' with Sandy Carmichael as the hero of the hour, having saved the hot water tank at the hotel from bursting at 4.00 a.m. and as a Scottish engineer he saved the 'ship' at the vital moment!

It was as warm and pleasant as ever in Pretoria and there can be few better climates in winter time. The Union Hotel, if old fashioned in some respects, has a friendly atmosphere. Actually, Pretoria as a whole, despite the hard rugby on the field at Loftus Versveld has a friendliness, warmth and hospitality from ambassadorial level down to the hotel staff, through the many sections of the city with special reference to the Northern Transvaal Rugby Union's staff; not forgetting the charming Rugby Magazine staff and the lunch to the touring Press Gang (South Africa and British Isles) was much appreciated with a ceremonial exchange of ties.

Air Vice Marshall Harold Hawkins entertained Vivian and myself at his beautiful new home and it was good to meet the late Alec de Villiers' son, Sandy, now an important banker in the City, for 'Uncle Alec' was our 'friend, guide and father confessor' in 1955 when Vivian and myself were aptly named the 'foreign press'. There was considerable tension in the city on the morning of the match and once again the 'Group' took to the fields and a picnic lunch in the warm sunshine. One felt that it was like playing a rugby match of importance at Stradey Park in midsummer but there was a touch of true challenge and danger in the air.

The Northern Transvaal has made seven changes, omitted their leading scrum-half, de Vos, and then had to take the field without their captain, Albert Bates, who was suffering from a chest injury. South African critics wondered whether the local selectors had gone too far in leaving out two Springboks, Tony Roux and de Vos, and had tempted fate, perhaps, too bravely. The Lions had to take the field without Phil Bennett, who was advised to rest his injured cartilage until the next match. The specialist told me it was a small cyst on the cartilage which would soon clear but that he should not be risked against Northern Transvaal. Although Bennett was disappointed, it was wise and necessary advice for a young man keen to play.

Match No. 16, at Loftus Versveld, Pretoria. July 6, 1974
British Isles defeated Northern Transvaal by one goal, two penalties and one try (16) to four penalties (12).
Crowd: 55,000. *Weather:* Sunny and warm. *Ground:* Firm with grass.
Scorers:
Northern Transvaal – C. Luther four penalties.

British Isles – T. M. Davies and A. Neary tries. A. R. Irvine one conversion and two penalties.
Teams:
NORTHERN TRANSVAAL: C. Luther; F. Aucamp, J. Knox, K. Kidson, H. Jacobs; V. Booyens, B. Van Wyk; N. Bezuidenhout, P. Van Wyk, H. Weber, J. Williams, M. Van Heerden, G. Eloff, C. Oosthuizen, T. Lourens (capt.).
BRITISH ISLES: J. P. R. Williams; A. R. Irvine, C. H. M. Gibson, R. A. Milliken, J. J. Williams; I. R. McGeechan, G. O. Edwards; J. McLauchlan, R. W. Windsor, F. E. Cotton, W. J. McBride (capt.), G. L. Brown, R. M. Uttley, T. M. Davies, A. Neary.
Referee: Mr P. Robbertze (Eastern Transvaal).

The crowd roared its approval when the teams fielded and roared even louder when the Northerns took the lead after five minutes. The Lions were up too quickly at a set scrum in defence and fell offside for Chris Luther to kick the first of his four penalty goals and put Northerns ahead. Irvine missed with two attempts and then put his third over from 28 yards to level the score when the Northerns were penalised at a line-out After 20 minutes the Northerns regained the lead when Neary fell offside at a line-out and Luther kicked a lovely goal from 45 yards but the Lions regained the lead in the 27th minute with a clever try.

They forced a line-out near the Northerns goal line following a fierce McBride charge and several five yard scrums that were hotly contested. Windsor threw a long ball to Mervyn Davies, whose famous 'cupped' hand gathered smartly at the top of the leap, and he came down to crouch and turn sharply through the line before diving over for a try that Irvine converted to make it 9–6. This appeared a lot healthier but there followed some good old-fashioned fisticuffs and a few boots before the interval, and both packs of forwards needed repairs. Booyens appeared to kick Davies on the ground in one short, sharp fierce, punch-up while Brown was booted in the backside. The referee spoke to the players, awarded a penalty to the Lions and though play continued to be extremely hard there were no more 'incidents' until near the end.

Resuming in the second half Andy Irvine failed with two penalty attempts from 45 and 48 yards before, after eight minutes play, the Lions were penalised at a collapsed scrum and Luther kicked his third goal from 54 yards to level the scores again. More than that, the penalty goal inspired the Northerns pack to raise their game and pound away to the roars of the crowd. They were challenging strongly but the Lions, ten minutes later, managed to force play with a sharp counter into the Northerns '25'. There they pushed the Northerns off the ball with a mighty effort and Edwards was away to the blind side where he fed J. J. Williams. He dashed ahead, jinked inside, and although he could well have got there himself, he wisely sent inside to Tony Neary who dived over for a good try.

Irvine could not convert this one by the Lions had the lead again and they were not to lose it, although two minutes later a fourth penalty goal by Luther really set the match alight. The Lions were penalised at a set scrum for not being straight and, as it was only 30 yards from the Lions goal line, it was a certain three points for the Northerns. At 13–12 the Lions were far from comfortable. Gordon Brown had his kick in the backside. Gareth Edwards twice caught at the back of scrum and ruck and the Lions good ball was getting less and less. Once Edwards and McGeechan had kicks charged down while from a ten yard scrum, Booyens kicked wide with a drop at goal. The pressure was really on!

The Lions' line kicks were still failing to reach their objective and the Northerns returned these with interest. After 38 minutes the death knell appeared to sound for the Lions. The ball was held and then released by them at a set scrum and Gareth Edwards appeared to dummy to gather as the Northerns scrum-half Van Wyk dashed offside. Edwards then went in to smother but was blown up for offside or something unusual as Referee Robbertze indicated that Edwards had kicked the ball back in when in actual fact the ball had not been touched. It was a sad moment. Luther lined up the kick which was well within his compass, only 30 yards out and, bang, it sailed wide and the Lions sighed with relief for that one certainly appeared to have their names written on it! The clock moved forward to injury time with the Lions still in the lead but by no more than a point and, surely, the Northerns could not snatch the match out of the fire at this stage, or was it the Lions turn to suffer a Bloemfontein?

The crowd was thirsting for victory now and wanted just one more effort from the Northerns as injury time was entered, but it was the Lions who countered to make the match safe. They moved the ball and when Milliken went racing up the left touch-line into the Northerns half he was stiff arm tackled by the enthusiastic but inexperienced (Number eight) Oosthuizen and laid out. Milliken had to be assisted from the field and Irvine took the penalty kick to strike a fine 47 yarder that made it 16–12. More injury time was played but the final whistle came with Edwards belting the ball high to touch and the Lions record was secure after 16 matches even if it had, for the second successive Saturday, been a 'close call'. One could almost hear the distant trumpets as the Northerns 'braves' pounded away against the Lions stockade. Hard, yes; exciting, yes; but spectacular – No!

Both sides had played ten man rugby with the Northerns putting everything into their forward effort. It almost paid off, but the character of the Lions, shone through, even during the hectic moments of desperate defence under severe pressure. The Northerns never looked like scoring a try and the Lions got two clever ones and, so, deserved to win. They realised they had not played as well as they should have done but much of their trouble was due to poor line kicking, and Syd Millar had no illusions about it. Even Gareth Edwards admitted he kicked badly and the side did not move the ball enough.

Vivian was adamant that the ball should have been moved more in counter attack in the 1971 manner, but there was difficulty on the part of the Lions in winning clean possession from line-out and rucks. John Williams, the Northerns lock, had a splendid match but the backs wasted a lot of ball with aimless kicking and Luther missed the vital place kick that could have given them an even better chance of victory. In the four matches following the Second Test the Lions had missed the 'little controller' Phil Bennett. The style of approach of the Quaggas, Free State, Griquas and the Northerns had all been different but had projected much hope for the future of the game in South Africa, since all four sides had shown fire and spirit. Their forward play had been more positive, while the Quaggas and Free State had possessed good halves, and the Griquas had attacked from half-back. The Northerns did well at forward and had they been met early in the tour, say the second match, then they could have won as, indeed, could the Free State but, by this time, even at the bottom of the graph of form the Lions were too well together, too good a team with character and guts. They would not yield!

CHAPTER EIGHT

The Third Test

At Pretoria there was a sense of relief, after the Northern Transvaal match, in the Lions' Camp that the 'fifth' test had been survived and the record was still intact, but the celebrations were reasonably quiet at the Union Hotel on the Saturday night and, following an early Sunday lunch, the rugby caravan moved on to East London and when the plane touched down at the coast again after seven matches on the highveld the players felt the atmosphere to be more humid, as the dryness and dust had gone, it was as if we had moved from one world to another. The welcome was indeed warm for in addition to the sun there were a few thousand enthusiasts to greet the Lions. Being Sunday afternoon there was a major turn out and the Africans were there full of gay laughter while a group of children sang and danced the 'hunting of the leopard' for their Lion guests.

East London is rather a sleepy town, one that has changed less than any other in South Africa and many friends of the last 25 years, Basil Kenyon, Dave Field and Len Parsons, were there to greet us. The Carlton Hotel had not changed, like the town, but many of the younger Lions would have enjoyed staying at one of the more modern seafront hotels where the Lions supporters were accommodated. A query was raised and the answer came, 'Rugby teams always stay at the Carlton.' Yet the hospitality of local officials and followers was warm and the Lions drove into the Mdantsane Stadium, 13 miles from the centre of the town, to train on the Monday. The team was announced with Phil Bennett in it and Gareth Edwards at scrum-half because John Moloney pulled a thigh muscle in training. McBride had to play instead of the injured Gordon Brown and there were four test players in action.

The Africans were called the 'Leopards' and had recently returned from their first overseas tour, to Italy, and were expected to offer reasonable opposition. On arrival at the township we soon sensed the atmosphere of friendly combat and the Stadium was a good one with an excellent playing surface. There were 15,000 present including 500 whites who required special tickets and passes to watch the match, and it was a change to see the Africans running their own match. A smart group of drum majorettes did some marching to the rhythm of a lively band and from the Press Box, high at the back of the stand, an excellent view was presented and even the telex post office machines were along side. What more could one ask?

Match No. 17, at Mdantsane Stadium, East London. July 9, 1974.
British Isles defeated African Leopards by five goals, two penalties and five tries (56) to two penalties and a try (10).
Crowd: 15,000. *Weather:* Sunny and warm. *Ground:* Firm with grass.
Scorers:
African Leopards – C. Mgweba one try; N. Mbiko two penalties.
British Isles – T. O. Grace(3), C. M. H. Gibson(2), G. O. Edwards, A. Morley, A. G. Ripley, A. R. Irvine and T. David tries. A. R. Irvine two penalties and five conversions.
Teams:
SOUTH AFRICAN LEOPARDS: V. Mnqatu; T. Tsotsobe, B. Mryazi, M. Mayomela, C. Mgweba; P. Swarts, N. Mbiko; V. Sonjani, T. Magxala (capt.), M. Maqosha, L. Ntshongwana, S. Yakayi, P. Matyeshana, V. Nakani, M. Cushe.
BRITISH ISLES: A. R. Irvine; T. O. Grace, I. R. McGeechan, C. M. H. Gibson, A. Morley; P. Bennett, G. O. Edwards; A. B. Carmichael, K. W. Kennedy, M. A. Burton, W. J. McBride (capt.), C. W. Ralston, T. David, A. G. Ripley, S. A. McKinney. Uttley replacement for Ralston second half.
Referee: Mr S. Strydom (Orange Free State).

Edwards burst over after three minutes to the openside of a five yard scrum to register the first of the Lions ten tries scored in the match and Irvine converted with an excellent kick, but although the Lions shoved the Leopards repeatedly off the ball at the set scrums and won ruck after ruck that enabled them to run about the field at will and launch continuous attacks, they could not pierce the defence easily. Twenty minutes elapsed before they scored again, and it was Tom Grace who dashed over after a movement started by a Ralston charge. Irvine converted and then kicked a beautiful 50 yard penalty.

For another ten minutes the Leopards held firm before Mbiko landed a penalty to rouse an excited crowd who were generous in their applause of the Lions as well as their own heroes. Alan Morley, playing in his first match of the tour, got his first try which was not converted and at the interval it was 17–3 to the Lions. This was an indication of the speed in cover defence of the Leopards, as the Lions won so much good possession only to spoil it by too many players wanting to do it all on their own and two of the chief offenders were Ripley and David who should have distributed more readily.

The Leopards had good defenders in back row forwards Cushe and Nakani while Mbiko was a lively worker at scrum-half and the two wings, Tsotsobe and Mgweba, who were ready to kick and chase whenever the opportunity came their way. Starved of possession from set pieces, rucks and mauls, the Leopards had to wait for the dropped pass or kick-on before countering. Obviously, they love kicking the ball and chasing after and their tackling was good, harder and cleaner than the Coloured Proteas in Cape Town.

The match was played in good spirit except for one unusual incident in the second half, after five minutes had elapsed, as suddenly prop Maqosha landed a punch full on the side of Ralston's jaw, pole-axed him and caused him to be carried from the field with blood pouring from a gaping wound. It was sudden, and as a local paper called it, rather unwisely I thought, 'a sweet punch', but later investigation revealed that the wrong player had been hit and it was another Lion who had been pulling Maqosha's jersey at the line-out. Normally, the Lions would have 'climbed in' with suitable retaliation but, on this occasion, and wisely too, McBride gave no signal for action, and later he told me, 'It was not the time or place to start a 'battle' between blacks and whites, although we resented the vlow on Chris Ralston. It was an isolated incident in an excellent match.'

It was an excellent match and everyone was pleased at the admirable control shown by the Lions in the circumstances as Ralston had a sore face for several days, although it did not prevent him from enjoying his cigar. I do believe he smoked more per day than myself! He was rushed to hospital and had four stitches inserted in his cheek, this following the day after he had an abcessed tooth removed. It was not his week!

In the second half the Lions scored at regular intervals as they applied intense running pressure, while Tom Grace really stretched his legs in the scoring of four tries. First Irvine kicked a penalty and then followed tries by Ripley, Gibson, Grace, Irvine, Grace, Gibson and David with Irvine converting four. Mbiko kicked his second penalty half way through the half, and then Mgweba completed an enterprising Leopards movement with a spectacular run and dive to the left corner for a worthy try and the crowd erupted. It was great stuff for them and the Press Gang. At the end, it was 56–10 but the Leopards had not been disgraced.

Andy Irvine with 20 points and an excellent match had won the race to the 100 points with his five conversions, two penalties and a try, and one felt then that he was bidding strongly for a test place, especially as Bennett was a doubtful starter even though he had played in this match. Told to take care of himself and avoid direct 'confrontation', he did just that, and did not do any kicking with his injured right leg. Yet if he was to play in the vital third test, he had to appear in this match, if only to get the 'feel' of things, and he escaped without further injury, although many were not convinced that he was one hundred per cent fit. He told me he was satisfied and that another three days would see him right. I felt he would play because he wanted so much to do so, and that mind would succeed over matter!

The announcement of the test team had to be delayed as Alun Thomas pointed out there were several alternatives depending upon Bennett's fitness, and it was delayed until Thursday. Meanwhile, on Tuesday evening Pat and Basil Kenyon entertained Vivian and myself to dinner and afterwards at their home, where I have stayed on previous tours, together with 'Stan the Pies and Id the coal,' two Welsh friends of ours and their wives, who have followed rugby, Wales and the Lions, all over the world. Idris Thomas is president of Bridgend R.F.C. and Stan Thomas, a well-known Cardiff supporter. We talked a great deal about rugby and Basil still held vivid memories of the 1951 Springboks side that he led until his eye injury and is ever grateful for the treatment he received in the British Isles, while his affection for

British rugby and the 1955 Lions has not weakened over the years.

On our return to Port Elizabeth on the Wednesday, the weather was perfect but one felt the test atmosphere, and almost immediately Syd Millar had the Lions in action at Boet Erasmus engaged in light training. We chatted to charming Mrs Marie O'Connell the E.P.R.U. secretary, and the Union's slightly 'wicked' chairman, Lawton Fourie, a friend of many, many years, while Mannie Katz was as kindly and considerate as ever, as the Press liaison officer. This time we had to stay at the Beach Hotel instead of the much loved Marine, and although it was comfortable and quiet, the Beach could not provide the menu of the Marine. Yet one could work without interruption at the Beach and receive telephone calls from the *Western Mail* asking for more and more copy!

Cas de Bruyn was nominated from a panel of four referees for the test but once again the list omitted Max Baise, although the Lions management had suggested to the South African Board that his name be included on the panel. If he was good enough to be on the panel for the first test and be selected, why not on the other two panels? This was one only the Board could answer but, it defeated their own admission that only their best referees would be on the panels. Some of the referees named had no chance of a test and so the choice of the Lions was limited but as Mr de Bruyn had done a good job in the second test, he was rightly awarded the third, although I know this did not exactly please certain Board members!

Then, on Thursday, Alun Thomas announced the Lions' side on the field at Boet Erasmus as the test side trained and Phil Bennett was in and so there was only one change, on the right wing, where Andy Irvine replaced his countryman, Billy Steele. It was not an easy choice but whereas Steele had lost a little of his sharpness in attack due to bruised ribs Irvine had improved steadily since his first few difficult matches, and had to be included in case Bennett should suffer further injury and be forced to leave the field. The side met with general approval and although Bennett did not kick in practice, he ran well and, as they say in New Zealand, 'propped' or side stepped without any obvious handicap.

Fresh from the UK were Albert Agar, John Law and Gordon

Rowley, and they studied the practice in the sun closely, as did thousands of others 'in the city for the test' including 150 Welsh supporters. With this party were Bleddyn Williams, Clem Thomas, Stan Bowes, Trevor Jones, Bryn Evans and other well-known figures in Welsh rugby while three more London rugby writers were on the job, in John 'the Greatest' Reed, Barry Newcombe and Douglas Ibbotson, to swell the Press Gang. Was it to be the 'kill' and a historic day or were the wounded Springboks to fight back and delay decision day until the last match of the tour? The Springboks selectors had made ten changes and were forced to make another as scrum-half Roy McCallum withdrew after being chosen, which was bad luck for him as he is the best in his position in South Africa. They tried out three, Sonnekus, Wolmarans and Schutte in training and, in the end, chose Sonnekus because he was Jackie Snyman's partner in the Free State side's good performance, although he was comparatively new to the scrum-half position, having previously played at flank forward and, unknown to the selectors, it was a fateful decision.

The Lions did not practice on Friday and I took a taxi to broadcast to the BBC from the SABC studios some miles out of the city, with Terry O'Connor and Alun Williams. The taxi driver lost his way half a dozen times, and I was able only to answer a few short questions put to me by Peter Jones, an able interviewer like Dennis Lyneham, while Cliff Morgan, as expert and as interested as ever, guided us so easily and so well. How we missed him on this tour since he is such a happy travelling companion with an insatiable interest in rugby football, sport in general, and people. The 'Fizzers' of 1968 were never quite the same without their liveliest member but by speaking to him every week and passing on odd titbits of gossip that could not be broadcast, kept him in touch with the party. During the tour he received a well deserved promotion to the post of Head of BBC Sound Outside Broadcasting and the Lions were delighted at the news.

Dewi Griffiths, Alun Williams and Nigel Starmer-Smith were lively enough on tour but, invariably, they travelled by car and lived at other hotels. In 1971 Mogs, Jenks and JBG were always together, aided and abetted by James the Mirror, to earn the title from their English colleagues of the 'Welsh Mafia'. This time the Press Gang was highlighted by the activities of the 'Noisy Boys', Messrs Smith, Lander and O'Connor!

Saturday morning dawned perfectly, with a warm sun shining out of a cloudless sky down upon the blue waters of Algoa Bay where the breakers sparkled in the morning sunlight. Yet it did nothing to ease the tension of the occasion, this was the big one, and travelling to the ground one felt more like a cricket reporter proceeding to a test match at Port Elizabeth than a rugby writer heading for the most important rugby test in South Africa for 64 years.

The ground was packed to capacity for the final curtain raiser that was really an unofficial trial match for the Springboks selectors, between the Junior Springboks and South African Universities, and such was the nature of the open play that one felt that apart from really good tight forwards, there were plenty of promising young players in the country. It was the blending that was difficult and soon this match was over and the main contestants took the field to rousing cheers. Obviously, it was going to be a 'battle to the death' for the Lions wanted to clinch the series and the Springboks were equally determined to win and attempt to share the series and avoid their worse rugby disaster since the start of the century.

Match No. 18. The Third Test at Boet Erasmus, Port Elizabeth. July 13, 1974.

British Isles defeated South Africa by one goal, two penalties, two dropped goals and two tries (26) to three penalties (9).

Crowd: 55,000. ***Weather:*** Warm and sunny. *Ground*: Firm and grassy.

Scorers:

South Africa – J. Snyman three penalties.

British Isles – G. L. Brown, J. J. Williams(2) tries; P. Bennett two dropped goals; A. R. Irvine one conversion and two penalties.

Teams:

SOUTH AFRICA: O. A. Roux (NT); G. H. Muller (Tvl), P. A. Cronje (Tvl), J. J. Schlebusch (OFS), C. F. Pope (WP); J. C. P. Snyman (OFS), D. Sonnekus (OFS); N. S. E. Bezuidenhout (NT), J. F. B. van Wyk (NT), J. F. K. Marais (EP) (capt.), J. de Bruyn (OFS), J. L. van Heerden (NT), J. T. Fourie (SET), J. L. Fritzinger (Tvl), J. H. Ellis (SWA).

BRITISH ISLES: J. P. R. Williams (W); J. J. Williams (W), R. A. Milliken (I), I. R. McGeechan (S), A. R. Irvine (S); P. Bennett (W), G. O. Edwards (W); F. E. Cotton (E), R. W.

Windsor (W), J. McLauchlan (S), W. J. McBride (I) (capt.), G. L. Brown (S), R. M. Uttley (E), T. M. Davies (W), J. F. Slattery (I).
Referee: Mr C. de Bruyn (Transvaal).

The Springboks set off at a cracking pace, giving it everything they had, and soon the Lions were on the defensive and the Springboks were almost over, forcing a five yard scrum, but the Lions won the ball for Bennett to clear. So sharp was their marking and spoiling that Edwards had two touch-line relieving kicks charged down and the crowd roared its appreciation. Here was a real South African challenge . . . the Lions would not have it all their own way! After four minutes the Lions were caught lifting at a line-out and Jackie Snyman made no mistake with his kick at goal from 25 yards. First blood, and important blood, to the Springboks which inspired them to go in much harder. It was 'boots and saddle' work in the Lions '25' and every item of tour drill was tested to the full in defence. The words of McBride kept ringing in my ears as I waited, high in the stand, for the first phone call from Cardiff, 'There can be no escape!', and for a while his proud team had their backs to the wall. This was its River Marne. They had to keep their line intact.

Bennett countered a little with rolling kicks to Tony Roux who was unsteady at first but after 15 minutes play the Springboks were penalised at a set scrum 48 yards out and Irvine with care and precision kicked a lovely high, soaring goal that gladdened the fast beating hearts of the Lions' camp followers. Ring, ding, ding, went my telephone and I was able to report all square at three-all. It could have been worse for the Springboks were hammering away and the Lions were tested to the full. Make no mistake about it; having set a cracking pace, the Springboks did not spare themselves but Sonnekus was slightly nervous and Snyman not too happy in the heat of the struggle. The Lions were standing firm and in the engine room, McLauchan, Windsor and Cotton were as solid as ever, and Brown and McBride were holding their own at the line-out. Slattery was away like a cannonball, harassing Snyman and company, while Davies, the master number eight, was here, there and everywhere, and Uttley, the unseen, unobtrusive Uttley, was deep in the mauls and rucks, working away.

McBride was holding them together with a word here, a pat there, and a close watch on the opposing eight, together with a nod or two to Gareth Edwards. Pre-match training, organisation and discipline held the line together and there was no Springbok break out. The Springboks tried their hardest; harder than in the first two tests, and one felt they would burst at the seams so vigorous was their effort then, suddenly, 'Whoosh', as Ray Prosser used to say, the fists began to fly. Ten players or more were involved and in the thick of it was the full-back, J. P. R. Williams, and he let fly to crack 'Moaner' van Heerden a nasty blow. Why? J.P.R. showed me his back on Sunday morning and he had been well and truly 'scraped' after the ball had gone. Order was eventually restored and a scrum formed with a Lions put in. Would it develop into a free-for-all. Was this test series; so important and, until now, cleanly played going to spoil the long series of happy but hard matches between the countries? There were anxious moments but although the tension remained there was no further outburst during the first half. More important however was the fact that the Lions took the lead in the third minute of injury time after five minutes of attacking in which they turned the Springbok tide. The fire died away a little and the Springbok steam was reduced in pressure, and as I was on the phone at the time to Cardiff I could hear the cheers in the background from the 'Echo' staff as the Lions went into the lead they were not to loose.

The Lions moved away and the much underrated Ian McGeechan made a clever break moving right. He kicked away to the corner and Irvine, following up at speed, steered the ball to touch near the right corner flag for a Springbok throw-in. Gordon Brown moved up the line from No. 5 to the front and, as the ball was thrown in fast and hard to the short line by Van Wyk, the clever Brown jumped high, gathered and dived over the line before you could say 'Boet Erasmus'. It was his eighth try of the tour to set a record for touring lock forwards and one of intense value to the Lions at this stage of the match. Irvine was wide with his kick at goal but the Lions changed ends in the lead at 7–3 and soon after the second half restarted there came the score that really tore the heart out of the Springboks effort since, until then, they had done well at forward with Hannes Marais having his best match of the series.

Their backs, especially the halves had not been too happy but Roux at full-back was ready to counter attack and Cronje appeared as a more than useful centre. After six minutes play the Springboks infringed following a mini line-out just inside the Lions half, and McBride called up Irvine to try his luck from 58 yards. With a superb kick he landed the longest penalty goal, or indeed, any goal of the series and at 10–3 the Lions were heading for victory and the series.

Irvine, now starting what could be a long career in test rugby, will not kick many better goals and one sensed the easing of the pressure upon the Lions but there followed another fierce punch up after 'Moaner' van Heerden had floored Bobby Windsor with a wicked punch and dashed away. Eventually, the flurry of punches ceased after the mêlée had moved from the '25' to the goal line in the Springboks half of the field. At the given signal the Lions moved in to retaliate as Windsor was a particularly popular member of the side and they would not stand by and see him punched, so it was lively for 20 seconds, but order was restored and Sonnekus was allowed to take the mark he had made, prior to the punch.

The Lions were now gaining control and playing extremely well. Another score had to come and from a scrum twenty yards out, after the ball had been held for a moment, Davies released it for Edwards to send a long pass to the waiting Bennett, who had time enough to drop a neat 25 yard goal and make it 13–3. Slowly and surely the score was moving away from the Springboks and the margin was growing wider so as to suggest little hope of recovery.

The Lions pack drove and harassed; won and held the ball at the set scrums, before delivering with timely precision to Edwards. They won more good ball at the line-out, drove into the rucks as a unit and slipped cleverly from the mauls. They were in control; giving a text book lesson in modern forward play, and providing every chance for Edwards and Bennett to control. Edwards always relished such a situation with puckish delight while Bennett, moved on his toes, was eager for work, aided by Doctor Kennedy's pain killing injection that set him free to run and kick.

The Springboks were now under severe pressure and sighed with relief when an Edwards attempt at dropped goal sailed wide but they still disposed themselves untidily to deal with Bennett's probing diagonal kicks. The open side wings still failed to stand deep and ease the burden of an active full-back, Roux. South Africa were playing the game the old-fashioned way, when they had continuous control at forward. They were not accustomed to being turned, but turned they were, and after 24 minutes it was 'All the way with J.J.' and a try of the highest quality to establish the Lions superiority with a touch of class and authority. From then on the series, deservedly, belonged to the 1974 Lions.

The Lions won a line-out some 45 yards out and moved to the left. Bennett missed out McGeechan as J. P. R. Williams joined the line. He and Milliken interpassed and J. J. Williams shot inside at top speed to take the inside pass and dart away like the Welsh 'whippet' he is, to end up between the posts for a superb try, it was a beauty. In the left corner were seated the 150 Welsh supporters and they immediately struck up 'Sospan Fach' which could be heard in the press box on the other side of the field!

Irvine kicked an easy goal and at 19–3 there was 'no escape' for the Springboks, now heading for defeat for the first time in the Port Elizabeth in 64 years, and one felt sympathy for them but the Lions had lost there in 1955 when the series was almost within their grasp. This time the grip merely closed tighter and there was nothing Marais could do to break out of it. Snyman kicked two fine penalty goals, each from 45 yards, but these were no more than gestures of defiance. The Springboks just could not break down the superb Lions cover when in possession and the pressure was so severe in front as to force them into errors. The heat was really on!

It was 19–9 and then after 39 minutes J. J. Williams scored another try, scorching the turf as he moved. J. P. R. Williams gathered a Springboks kick-on ten yards outside his own '25' and moved away to his left. After making some ground he handed on to Dick Milliken, who drew a man inside the Springbok half and fed left wing Williams who accelerated as two Springbok defenders closed him. Then a shrewd kick on while running at top pace sent the ball rolling down the touch line, before bouncing up to him as his eyes flashed with joy, he was away. No one would catch him now and as his brother, Ken, in the left corner, captured the exciting moment with his cinecamera, J.J. went diving over for his second try.

The Springboks knew they had been mastered, and Bennett's second dropped goal in injury time was the coup de grâce. Edwards moved to the blind side of a set scrum after waiting like a postman for Mervyn Davies to open the door and release the ball. The defence was drawn perfectly and then Edwards sent a reverse pass for Bennett to pouch, set his sights on the upright, and let go. It was a perfect dropped goal and made the score 26–9. Enough, and Cas de Bruyn blew his whistle. The field was invaded. The Lions hoisted their mighty captain, all smiles, to their tired shoulders, and marched off the field like conquerors. They were, since their achievement had not been accomplished by any team this century.

One was almost hoarse with delight sending the last words of the 'Echo' report to Cardiff and Mrs Leighton, an excellent copy taker, thoroughly enjoyed it all, while one must say 'Thank you' to telephone engineers and operators along the line. There have been fewer happier rugby stories that I have phoned to Cardiff in nearly thirty years. The British Isles Rugby Union team, disowned by its government, had achieved a tremendous victory in becoming the first Lions side to beat South Africa in a series since 1896. More important still, it had become the first side to win a series in South Africa this century.

The crowd applauded warmly as the Lions walked off in a genuine show of appreciation and this was symbolic of the pleasure the side had given to all South Africans, and especially the coloured people who had remained steadfast in their support. The South African members of the Press Gang were ready and warm in their congratulations even though a few of them, in the days that followed, castigated the national selectors rather overpoweringly, and 'Sniped' at the Lions for their prologned celebrating!

Thousands of words were typed and written in the Press Box at Boet Erasmus in the hours that followed the end of the match and several poured words over the air into the British Isles, everywhere the news was almost instant. The Lions were the new world champions at rugby football. In 1891 the news of an unbeaten record had to be carried from Cape Town to Southampton by ship but now, 83 years later, and a complete change in the way of life of Africa, another side looked like enjoying or achieving an unbeaten tour.

The evening saw the celebrations start and continue right through until Sunday night and the early hours of Monday morning. Some beer was spilled on the carpets and one fire extinguisher used in a 'charge' but considering the occasion and the size of the celebrations, which included the consumption of 65 bottles of champagne, this was indeed little damage. It was paid for immediately to the hotel owners by manager Thomas and amounted to R300 while the hotel owner said, 'We are not unduly concerned as none of the damage was serious.' Actually it was 5.00 a.m. on Sunday morning when the celebrations reached their height but I can say, that I have known far more damage done in the distant days of the past when the Lions were not victorious. As the hotel owner said, 'We'll welcome the Lions back, anytime, as there was no unpleasantness during their two stays with us and they are a fine rugby side.'

When Monday morning came, Syd Millar had them out working in the hot sun, and there were a few 'fat' heads while one player claimed, 'This horse is unfit for work,' and admitted that every lap of the field sent extra pain shooting through his head. The plane set off from Port Elizabeth to East London on time but as it was climbing over Algoa Bay, a bird was sucked into the port jet engine and, immediately, we heard the engine pitch change, the pilot levelled off, and moved in a wide circle to line up for landing on one engine. Captain Pieter Erasmus executed a perfect landing and the plane came to a halt outside the airport buildings. 'That was a short trip,' commented one Lion, but three of them, Bobby Windsor, Chris Ralston and Stewart McKinney said, 'Enough for one day, we'll go by hired car!' and they received permission to do so. There was a four hour delay while another 737 was sent for from Johannesburg and the journey to East London completed. The 'battle' of Boet Erasmus was over, but one should not call it a 'battle', but rather a show of British Rugby strength as the Lions had won well and convincingly with good rugby.

CHAPTER NINE

The Fourth Test

The South African press were full of praise for the Lions on Sunday and Monday and Dr Craven called them the 'Greatest team to visit South Africa' in his speech at the after-match reception in the Port Elizabeth town hall. It was generous praise from a great rugby man, but the truth, as they had proved themselves the greatest. Several of the unsuccessful teams between 1896 and 1974 had contained outstanding and brilliant players but none had played as well together as this one, and both English and Afrikaans newspapers splashed the accolade 'Greatest' in their headlines and it gave one a sense of pride even as an observer to have shared in this Odyssey.

Good management, wise coaching and dedicated captaincy with one hundred per cent loyalty from the players made all this possible on tour and it was a just reward for five years of solid effort by clubs and unions in the British Isles in devoting time to coaching and training and a much more comprehensive study of the game than has ever been undertaken by any country. The power and control of the scrummaging was the first solid brick in the foundation of a successful team and this sense of tactical and technical appreciation was carried right through from Ian McLauchlan at loose-prop to John Williams, towering above all other full-backs.

South Africa did a great deal of soul searching after this match and the selectors came under fire from the press but it went a great deal deeper than mere selection. In the first place, the Lions had outstanding players in key positions and a magnificent leader and, secondly, their standard of team work developed by playing together and employing modern coaching techniques, was superior to a Springboks side attempting to find its feet and blend together as a team.

Their selectors may have had a 'rush of blood' after the First

Test and made too many changes for the second, but the first half of the Third Test indicated that they were getting somewhere with their pack of forwards. The great need was five players of strength, quality and fire in the front five, and this was something that is, normally, very much a part of South African rugby at international level. It was, for the selectors, a matter of trial and error, until the final test.

One of the nicest couples in East London are Pat and Basil Kenyon who extend the warmest of welcomes and early on Tuesday morning Basil, Alun Thomas, Vivian Jenkins and myself, set off for the Transkei to enjoy one of the happiest 'off duty' days of the tour. A pleasant drive took us to a trading post beyond Butterworth where Len Muller and family welcomed us and introduced us to the 'mysteries' of the business done with the natives on such friendly terms. We three Welshmen were fascinated and Vivian commented, 'The whole of the British Cabinet should fly out and see this!' Then on to visit several rondavels and meet happy African people, for they were happy while they danced before us.

Even the elderly matrons danced but we were more amused at the menfolk who sat down and allowed all the women to do the work while they smoked traditional Xhosa pipes and drank beer from large plastic mugs. Here were Africans as they have lived for thousands of years and were far happier than many groups of European communities we met along the way. As Vivian said, 'What a place for retirement; no wonder they live a long time; simply nothing to worry about!' Then on to Butterworth and a visit to the modern factories that have been built for the people of the Transkei, one of the first Bantustans, for them to run themselves in due course. The sack factory was the most modern in the world and having last visited the Transkei in 1962, I saw much to please me this time and, as all peaceful change in Southern Africa will be gradual, then progress was being made, but the outside world remains impatient.

On Wednesday, the 19th match of the tour was played against Border in East London and a pleasant lunch with Mr and Mrs Ben Parsons recalled the happy days of 1955, and the famous Lions party at the Duggans when every gent was afraid to visit the 'loo' because there was a life-size 'dummy' astride the seat.

Again, the Duggan's home was the place were Vivian told the 'Milkman' story to the senior members of the Cambrian Society in 1962, and where John Reed first learned the dance of the Transkei as well as the place where Border won in 1955, and where some 'unknown' reporter really went to town against the 'wreckers and burners' of 1968. Little did we know beforehand that another 'unknown' was to repeat history and prove even more fictional this time, causing a great deal of distress to the Lions management and the players as well as disturbing the equilibrium of the press gang.

Match No. 19 at the B.R.U. Ground, East London. July 17, 1974.
British Isles defeated Border by one goal, four penalties and two tries (26) to two penalties (6).
Crowd: 15,000. *Weather:* Sunny and windy. *Ground:* Very hard.
Scorers:
British Isles – W. C. C. Steele(2), G. O. Edwards tries, A. R. Irvine four penalties, one con.
Border – J. Steenekamp two penalties.
Teams:
BORDER: P. Venter; A. Stephenson, M. Harper, E. Van der Linde, T. Kotze; R. Gendall, J. Steenekamp; T. Schutte, W. Hattingh, J. Vos, S. Woods, G. Barter, G. Willson, K. Watt (capt.), D. Neale-May.
BRITISH ISLES: A. R. Irvine; T. O. Grace, R. T. Bergiers, C. M. H. Gibson, W. C. C. Steele; I. McGeechan, G. O. Edwards (capt.); A. B. Carmichael, K. W. Kennedy, M. R. Burton, C. W. Ralston, R. M. Uttley, S. A. McKinney, A. G. Ripley, T. P. David.
Referee: Mr G. Bezuidenhout (Transvaal).

This was a scrappy match, hampered by a strong wind blowing down the ground that considerably effected handling and kicking. The Lions did not play all that well against a brave Border side dedicated to spoiling and the keeping of the score to reasonable proportions, an attitude that could not be criticised since by this stage of the tour, the weaker provinces did not wish to lose by heavy margins, when they realised they had little opportunity of beating the Lions. Border relied upon continuous tackling and covering, as instructed by former Springbok captain and tactician, Basil Kenyon, who told me on Monday before the match that he had advised every Border player to 'tackle, tackle and still tackle'. And this they did.

Thus, considering the possession the Lions received, but not all of it good, the Border defence did well to limit the number of Lions tries to three. They conceded four penalties goals and kicked only two themselves when they should have kicked at least two more in an undistinguished match. The Lions wings were not at their best although Steele was hampered by a cracked rib sustained in the first half, and played on bravely until 10 minutes from time, when he was replaced by J. P. R. Williams. Andy Irvine, as ever, was in good form as a running full-back and a place kicker, collecting another 14 points with five goals, and looking the most improved young back in the party with an insatiable enthusiasm for the game.

The Border back row of Neale-May, Watt, the captain, and Willson, played extremely well and so did scrum-half Gendall, while the three-quarters tackled well, but they could not win enough possession against a heavier and stronger Lions pack that did not blend quite as well as it should have done. Once again, one felt that the Lions towards the end of the tour revealed a tendency, when obtaining ready possession at forward, to play with less cohesion than they did against stronger opposition. Perhaps, this is understandable towards the end of a long tour, when the test XV is settled and most of the other players do just enough to ensure comfortable victory. Edwards was leading the side but he, too, tried too hard himself, as he often did when not partnered by Bennett. The three back row forwards, David, Ripley and McKinney, also tried too much on their own, and while the individual efforts were often good and made ground, the Lions should have scored more points in the first half, when they changed ends at 10–3. Irvine kicked two penalties and Steele got a try while Steenekamp kicked one goal in three attempts for Border.

Yet the Lions added another record to their 'bag' by scoring three tries as they left the 1955 record of 94 tries behind, while Irvine with 14 points nosed in front of J. F. Byrne, of blessed memory, of 1896 who had held his record of 127 points for nearly eighty years. Again, the Lions made inroads into the All Blacks all-comers points record of 687 in 1970, which they were to pass in the match against Eastern Transvaal. Thus it was an interesting day if not a spectacular one.

In the second half Steele got his second try, a good one, and Edwards charged over for one from a ten yard scrum. Irvine kicked two penalties and one conversion and Steenekamp got a second penalty for the Border to see the match end at 26–6 and the Lions remain unbeaten, with three matches to go for a brilliant record. After the match the reception was enjoyable and amusing in the pleasant clubhouse below the stand while the pressbox had proved comfortable during the afternoon. I spent some time talking to Ian Kirkpatrick and Basil Kenyon about selection and found Ian most ready to talk, off the record, of the trials and tribulations of selection at a time when South Africa lacked the quality key players possessed by the Lions. One could not but agree that J. P. R. Williams, Bennett, Edwards, Davies, McBride, Brown and McLauchlan would have helped the Springboks and turned the balance of power in their favour!

From East London we flew off to Durban and there were a few 'high jinks' during the night after the match but nothing serious although, after we have been in Durban for a day, the 'phantom scribe' struck again and sent a powerful piece to *Die Transvaler* on nude scrummaging which appeared on the Friday morning and was followed up by all other papers. The facts were vague but a long way from the truth, as became the 'gentleman' from East London who had hammered the Lions of 1968. A pleasant sleepy town with warm hearted officials, it was losing its appeal after this second outburst and, as one Lion said, 'We should stop playing there until this scribe is unfrocked!' On that Friday in Durban he had many supporters.

Actually, two Lions who, like many other young men, sleep without pyjamas in warm weather, were awakened by their team mates and they emerged into the hotel corridor with towels round their hips. These were snatched from them and their room doors slammed. Thus they were in 'splendid isolation' and they chased their team mates to get back their towels and send for keys. This 'skylark' was reported as corridor scrummaging between nude lions and girl friends. Slightly exaggerated, I would think. Then another player was 'visited' and his bed put out through an open window on to a balcony. So much for East London but by the time the team had reached Johannesburg again, the Carlton Hotel manager had written to Alun Thomas, telling him of the good behaviour of the party and that the Lions would always be welcomed. End of sensational story. What some scribes will do for money!

Alun Thomas and myself were guest speakers at the Duikers Annual Dinner in Durban on the Friday night where Colin Wesley, former South African test cricketer, was an excellent chairman. We entered into the convivial spirit of the evening and it was my pleasure to redraft the laws of the game to include 'nude scrummaging', and ensure that the scribe of East London was not taken seriously. The good rugby men of Natal were preparing for 'battle' as the 'last outpost of the Empire' and though lacking in weight were preparing some 'hot curry' for the Lions. Tommy Bedford, a former Springbok, is extremely popular in his own province, and everyone there thought he should have been given the Springbok captaincy before Hannes Marais but, obviously, the national selectors did not agree. So Bedford for one was ready to play the match of his life and as a result of the 'confrontation' the Lions hit the headlines again on Saturday night and Sunday!

Match No. 20 at King's Park, Durban. July 20, 1974.
British Isles beat Natal by three goals four penalties and a try (34) to two penalties (6).
Crowd: 38,000. *Weather:* Sunny. *Ground:* Firm and dry.
Scorers:
British Isles – A. R. Irvine(2), T. M. Davies and J. F. Slattery tries. P. Bennett three cons and four penalties.
Scorers:
Natal – K. Hannaford two penalties.
Teams:
NATAL: M. Swanby; R. Pitcher, R. Ferguson, P. de Lange, A. van der Watt; I. Healey, S. Holmes; T. Basson, J. Trollope, D. van der Berg, J. Kapp, J. de Kock, M. McKenzie, T. Bedford (capt.), H. Norton.
BRITISH ISLES: J. P. R. Williams; A. J. Morley, C. M. H. Gibson, R. A. Milliken, J. J. Williams; P. Bennett, G. O. Edwards; J. McLauchlan, R. W. Windsor, F. E. Cotton, W. J. McBride (capt.), C. W. Ralston, A. Neary, T. M. Davies, J. F. Slattery.
Referee: Mr P. Robbertse (Eastern Transvaal).

The final score in this match in no way reflects the tension, excitement, vigour, and the final magnificent flourish by the Lions, and the hard things said about the tourists when it was all over and the strange 'confrontation' between local hero Tommy Bedford and the world's No. 1 full-back, J. P. R. Williams, which produced unprecedented crowd scenes in the 'last outpost of the Empire'. Natal took a long time to crack, far longer than the Lions anticipated, but because of long and regular stoppages, there was eleven minutes of injury time and it was during this period that the Lions let rip, to produce some superb attacking football that overwhelmed an exceedingly brave and lighter Natal side. The Lions had to have a replacement for Morley with a bruised heel in the second half and he, Andy Irvine, collected two splendid tries, while Natal had to have two replacements, in Hannaford for van der Watt and Brocklehurst for Kapp at lock. Hannaford kicked two fine penalties and caused one to wonder why he was not selected in the first place.

Bennett put the Lions ahead after two minutes with a penalty goal following an infringement at a maul before Pitcher kicked wide with his first attempt for Natal and so keen was the forward play in the early stages that there appeared little chance of tries being scored. The Lions placed all emphasis upon forward play and drove hard in the loose as well as dominating the scrummaging while Natal tried to rush and slip the ball in their traditional way. Swanby at full-back was sound in defence but the Lions scrummaging pressure was an indication of what would follow eventually. Pitcher missed another kick at goal before Bennett kicked his second from 25 yards after Natal were penalised at a scrum for not straight, and then got his third goal after 33 minutes from 30 yards after a line-out infringement.

We thought then that this would have broken Natal's resistance but it was far from it, although they lost their big lock, Binky Kapp, with a leg injury. He had to be helped from the field and was replaced by prop Brocklehurst with Van der Berg moving to the lock position. Before the interval Swanby missed a kick at goal and it was just not Natal's day. Early in the second half Edwards was prominent with a drop at goal and then a charge over the line from a scrum for a try that was disallowed. Then Van der Watt pulled a hamstring and left the field to make way for the place kicking wing, Hannaford, before Morley retired with a bruised heel and Irvine joined the scene.

Hannaford kicked a penalty after 23 minutes and another one after 29 minutes to make it 9–6 and the whole match was alight. However, before these goals there were scenes. The first involved Bedford and J. P. R. Williams. The Natal captain kicked ahead and followed up and Williams did not gather cleanly. He was tackled by Bedford and intentionally or otherwise, Williams received a kick in back of head as the two players bundled into touch and then into the crowd. Williams lashed out at back of Bedford's head and had to be restrained by the crowd. Eventually, he returned to field to boos from the crowd and Bedford had to be revived as spectators threw oranges and ran on to the field.

It was a difficult moment and, eventually, Bedford returned to the field of play to the cheers of the partisan crowd. Understandably, he was their hero and only later was the truth learned, but after the match Williams spoke to Bedford and they shook hands. Then Bedford was 'felled' at a line-out, and again the crowd rushed on to the field while other spectators pelted the Lions with oranges and beer cans. McBride led his players to the centre of the field, away from 'hell fire' corner until police had restored order. Every time Williams was in contact with the ball he was booed, but it was six of one and half a dozen of the other for when he showed me the lump on the back of his head on the Sunday he said, 'I am not a dirty player but after getting the kick on the head, I lost my 'cool' and I am sorry. Anyway, we have spoken together and shaken hands and the incident is best forgotten.'

The local papers went to town and the *Sunday Tribune* called the Lions 'bully-boys' which was taking the matter too far. They were not, even though they refused to be intimidated. After 30 minutes of the second half, it was 9–6 to the Lions and then Natal cracked. They had done extremely well for 70 minutes but the many stoppages were to prolong injury time and when Irvine got his first try after 32 minutes, it was all over. From a line-out, followed by a maul, Edwards went blind and fed Irvine on the right wing and he ran well before beating three coverers and crossing for a splendid try. Bennett hit the post with his conversion attempt, but at 13–6 Natal had to submit, although never readily!

The Lions forwards took command and scored the first of their 'walked over' tries after 43 minutes through Mervyn Davies which Bennett converted, and these six points were the first of 21 points scored by the Lions in seven exciting minutes, when they raced from 13 to 34 points to rout Natal and leave a final score that contained little credit for the brave, vanquished local side, but demonstrated the superb forward power of the Lions.

A penalty was awarded to the Lions and Bennett popped it over from 32 yards, and then came another try from Andy Irvine, following a dazzling run by Bennett which he converted and, in the 49th minute of the second half, the Lions 'walked' the tired Natal pack again and when the Lions forwards crossed the goal line, the ball spurted out of the side of the scrum and after a moment's hesitation, Fergus Slattery fell on it for a try and Bennett kicked his seventh goal to bring his tally to 18 points for the match and pass his century for the tour.

Eventually, after 11 minutes of injury time the final whistle was blown and Natal carried their battered captain Tommy Bedford from the field, but his personal 'vendetta' against the South African selectors was far from finished. At the traditional reception to both teams and guests in a marquee on No. 2 ground, Bedford could not resist another 'crack' at Johaan Classen and his fellows and it is alleged, although I arrived too late from the Press Box to witness it, he gave the selectors the Churchillian sign, which was a little unbecoming such a famous player. Naturally, everything about Bedford was rather sad in the papers on Sunday and Monday, as it was not the right sort of publicity, but he may have been an outlet for provincial opinion that its rugby was being neglected by South Africa, generally, and he was used as battering ram.

I tried to ease the situation in the *Daily News* on the Monday as Danie Craven had done when speaking last at the reception in the marquee, since Natal needed South African rugby and South Africa needed Natal rugby. It was as simple as that, and one did not wish to see the 'crack of bitterness' widening. All was quiet at Durban on Saturday evening but many found it hard to leave the seaside resort on Sunday afternoon and head for Johannesburg or, as photographer Gert Hattingh called his home town, 'Swinging Joeys'. Cheerful Ralph Daniel, back from Japan, greeted Vivian and myself at Jan Smuts Airport and we had supper with his daughter and son-in-law, Roma and Tim. We were entering the last week of the tour and the minor duty jobs ahead of us assumed a frightening spectre that was to harass in no uncertain manner!

Monday was a chase about and I had a pleasant lunch with the chairman of the 1968 Group which caused considerable interest among the three pleasant travelling VIP's, Albert Agar, John Law and Gordon Rowley, while several friends visited the table to be introduced, not forgetting my good friend Ned, who cared for me during the tour, and saw that I never wasted any time and carried my typewriter or 'truth machine' as Paul Irwin called it, everywhere. Yes, Ned was a good pal on tour and almost gained admission to the Welsh 'Mafia' of Jenkins, Griffiths and Thomas, if not the 'Fizzers'.

On Tuesday we set off for Springs early with two good Welsh friends, Claude Davey, the outstanding Welsh captain of the 1930's, and Glyn Davies, who played for Swansea with Claude and who followed him into University, and who had not met each other for 40 years. Needless to report it was a happy reunion and Glyn first took us on a rapid tour of the only zinc works in South Africa, of which he is works manager, which we discovered produced over 200 metric tons per day. Then he gave two of his senior staff and we three Welshmen a splendid lunch at a French restaurant in Springs. The food was so enjoyable that I will never make any wise cracks about Springs again, even if Bert Woolley, another good friend, sent off John O'Shea there in 1968! John had hoped to fly over to South Africa for the last two matches of the tour, but was prevented from doing so by illness, and both he and former referee, Woolley, were upset about it as they correspond regularly.

Match No. 21 at Pam Brink Stadium Springs. July 23, 1974.
British Isles defeated Eastern Transvaal by two goals three penalties and three tries (33) to two penalties and a try (10).
Crowd: 25,000. *Weather:* Sunny with cold wind. *Ground:* Hard.,
Scorers:
British Isles – T. O. Grace(2), T. P. David, A. G. Ripley and I. R. McGeechan tries. A. R. Irvine three penalties two conversions.
Eastern Transvaal – G. Salt two penalties. K. Fourie try.

Teams:
EASTERN TRANSVAAL: D. van Rensburg; G. Salt, J. Els, H. Coetzer, W. Murray; B. Dercksen, L. Petersen; P. Bierman, R. McKechnie, L. Stander, N. McIntyre, C. Holthausen (capt.), K. Fourie, B. Wilkinson and B. Stander.
BRITISH ISLES: J. P. R. Williams (capt.); A. R. Irvine, R. T. E. Bergiers, I. R. McGeechan, T. O. Grace; C. M. H. Gibson, J. J. Moloney; A. B. Carmichael, K. W. Kennedy, M. R. Burton, C. W. Ralston, R. M. Uttley, T. P. David, A. G. Ripley, S. A. McKinney.
Referee: Mr S. Strydom (Orange Free State).

Unhappily, the Eastern Transvaal had acquired a reputation for being hard, spoiling 'knuckle' men, with 1968 and the sending off of John O'Shea, then a couple of rough matches during the season, including one with Tarbes which was abandoned 20 minutes from the end, although I am sure that it was as much the fault of Tarbes as it was that of Eastern Transvaal. Consequently, the Lions selectors were worried more than a little as they did not seek a physical 'confrontation' in the penultimate match of the tour which would produce possible injury to key test players. However, the Eastern Transvaal officials must have read the 'riot act' to their players as it proved to be one of the most enjoyable matches of the tour and the 'Wednesday' team turned in a most satisfactory performance that delighted the Easterns supporters and pleased the Lions.

The Easterns took an early lead through a place kicking wing, Salt, after two minutes from 52 yards before Irvine landed one from 48 yards. Then Irvine kicked one from 20 yards followed by another from Salt, and it was 6–6 to suggest a good challenge for the Lions, several of whom were playing their last match of the tour. Then Moloney sent Gibson to the blind side of a 20 yard scrum and the outside-half put Tom Grace over in the corner to score a try within the law of 'adjustment'. Irvine missed the conversion and then Salt attempted a penalty attempt from the half way line and was only just wide to indicate the Easterns were determined to keep up with the unbeaten Lions.

After 29 minutes the Lions moved well to the left, where Ripley burst away from a line-out and set up a maul five yards out from which David burst over for a try on the open side and Irvine converted. Salt was wide again with a penalty attempt before the interval when it was 16–6 to the tourists and another victory in sight. They made certain of no repetition of any 'cliff hanger' by playing remarkably well for the first 15 minutes of the second half, when they shook themselves free of any Wednesday 'tag' and played like Saturday men.

First Ripley went over from tight head scrum 10 yards out and Irvine converted and then away from a maul with another long striding burst after J. P. R. Williams had made some of the running and, finally, McGeechan finished it off with his first try of the tour, much to the delight of his colleagues. Irvine could not convert but soon landed a massive penalty goal from the half way line to show that he was taking the whole thing very seriously!

Then the Lions backs moved smartly from right to left and Grace scampered over for his 13th try, one ahead of J. J. Williams, and this was to remain the top try total of the tour. At this stage the Lions led 33–6 and appeared to ease a little following their purple patch, as if surprised by the real enjoyment they were obtaining from a clean, fast moving match. There followed attempts at penalty goal and Irvine, with the taste of success sweet, attempted one huge goal from 62 yards with his longest kick of the tour, and he was only just wide!

Jonker replaced an injured Els in the centre for the Easterns and in the last minute of actual time, following a period of pressure they took a short penalty ten yards out in the right corner and flanker Fourie charged over for a deserved try that was not converted. The match ended at 33–10 and both the locals and the Lions were delighted that the true image of Eastern Transvaal rugby had been restored. The press gang typed on in the cold, and it was cold! For an hour, without overcoats, we stuck it and Neil Cameron and myself were the last to join the reception, but by then the speeches had started and bar was closed. However, the room temperature rose quickly and normal circulation was restored.

In the coach back to Johannesburg, I sat with Bob Scott and we chatted about all things affecting rugby and were in complete agreement about the 1974 Lions. They were the best and most efficient we had seen. They did not have, perhaps, the high glamour of the 1950, 1955 and 1971 sides' back divisions but they had a better pack of forwards, better control, and drill plus tremendous team work, and all were devoted to the cause. Scott's words still ring in my ears, 'If you control the set scrums and loose ball on tour, you cannot go wrong. It is the very basis of all things.' We had watched it in South Africa and New Zealand for years, and now we were watching the Lions do it even better This in itself justified their being called the 'Greatest' as a team.

The next morning, Manager Thomas announced the test XV and, as anticipated, it did not include Gordon Brown or Mike Gibson. Despite his wish to play and attempt to get fit, medical opinion was against Brown playing, and although his absence was to prove a loss, it was the best and wisest decision, for one thought of poor Clive Rees and his broken finger with 'lightning' striking twice. Chris Ralston filled the vacancy to achieve his ambition of becoming a 'full' Lions and was only the 17th player called upon in the series; an indication of wise selection and teamwork.

Gibson was extremely disappointed at not making the test side, as he had hoped to win a place by doing his best in the seven matches he had played out of a possible nine. However, the selectors decided to retain the back division that had served them well in the tests and they concealed well the obvious worry concerning Bennett's knee and injured cartilage. It was far from right, but Bennett had to play. The side was far happier and, indeed, stronger with him in it and playing outside Edwards. One sensed that even the brilliant Edwards tried that bit too hard when Bennett was not there and the pattern of Bennett's kicking to the open in attack, and Edwards to the 'box', was an essential part of the 'penetration' plan.

The Lions had a good workout on Wednesday and Thursday mornings at Ellis Park, as did the Springboks under Johaan Classen at Springfields, where they appeared far more relaxed. To me this was a dangerous sign, for a relaxed side with nothing to lose spells trouble! They had selected a better side, especially at forward and it was not going to be easy for the Lions to 'lift' their game yet again, for the 22nd time, at the end of a long tour. Indeed, they were more vulnerable now, than at any time before the previous 21 matches.

Again, they had to pack and prepare for home, and in all my travels I have never seen as much stuff as these 1974 Lions had to return with, apart from their normal clothes and equipment. When Phil Bennett's copper table arrived poor Bobby Windsor, who was sharing a room with him, did not believe even a 747 would get off the ground with it. Masseur Dave Godfrey gave the team wonderful help with their packing and they were 'unsighted' on Thursday and Friday afternoons, getting rid of the 'rubbish'.

The end of a great tour was in sight, and the loyal Lions supporters crowded into the Landdrost Hotel, that had proved a friendly and helpful Jo'burg headquarters, all in search of tickets or, at least, better tickets. British supporters would not sit at home in temporary stands at £5 a time, but they really are keen on their rugby in South Africa. Saturday dawned clear, sunny and warm and the scene was set for the decider; an unbeaten record or not. If the Lions failed at the last hurdle; great would be the disappointment for them and their supporters, not to mention the good folk at home. They must not fall at the very last fence.

Match No. 22. The Fourth Test.
Played at Ellis Park, Johannesburg. July 27, 1974.
British Isles drew with South Africa scoring one goal, one penalty and one try (13) to three penalties and a try (13).
Crowd: 75,000. *Weather:* Sunny. *Ground:* Hard and dry.
Scorers:
South Africa – P. Cronje a try. J. Snyman three penalties.
British Isles – R. M. Uttley and A. R. Irvine tries. P. Bennett one con. Irvine one penalty.
Teams:
South Africa: O. A. Roux; G. Muller, P. Cronje, J. Schlebusch, C. Pope; J. Snyman, P. Bayvel; J. Bezuidenhout, P. Van Wyk, J. H. P. Marais (capt.), J. Williams, M. van Heerden, J. Kritziner, C. J. Grobler, J. H. Ellis. (J. Stander replaced Bezuidenhout in second half after 15 mins).
British Isles: J. P. R. Williams; J. J. Williams, R. A. Milliken, I. R. McGeechan, A. R. Irvine; P. Bennett, G. O. Edwards; J. McLauchlan, R. W. Windsor, F. E. Cotton, W. J. McBride (capt.), C. W. Ralston, R. M. Uttley, T. M. Davies, J. F. Slattery
Referee: Mr M. Baise (Western Province).

This fourth and final test proved what we expected it would be; a hard and exciting match, with the Springboks revealing a vast improvement but the Lions not proving as good or as strong as they had been in the first three tests. Both sides missed several chances apiece that would have won them the match and it ended on a controversial note, but the final score of 13 points to each side and the first draw of the tour was a just result. In their respective dressing rooms, the Lions were extremely disappointed at not winning while the Springboks were overjoyed with the draw, yet each country had achieved something. The Lions had remained unbeaten in 22 matches; a monumental feat in itself, and the Springboks had prevented a 'whitewash' in the test series, that would have proved a national disaster, and indicated that they could rebuild themselves into a much stronger side. Hannes Marais, the Springbok captain, could retire in peace rather than pieces, and well deserved to be carried from the field in honour, while the five selectors could, once again, sleep at nights and put an end to the rude letters and phone calls, while their devoted wives would find the daily routine of shopping and coffee parties less arduous!

The Lions recovered sharply when they realised that only one Lions' side, that of 1891, had ever gone through an overseas tour unbeaten, and they attended the reception to listen to the many generous and sincere words of praise showered upon them. Willie McBride visited the SABC commentary box before he left the ground at Ellis Park, probably for the last time, and chatted to his wife and two children, invited to Broadcasting House in London by Cliff Morgan. Then he emerged and told me, 'It would have been nice to have won and I believe we scored a last minute try, but we have completed the tour unbeaten and that's history now!' He smiled, puffed at his pipe, and moved on with a shrug of his huge shoulders. At that moment McBride was a big man, a proud man, but still a cheerful and normal, natural man, untouched by the great success he had done so much to ensure. The game will find another McBride, perhaps, but not easily as they come no better.

There were cheers for the teams and greatest cheer from the 'richest' rugby crowd in history when the Springboks took the lead after five minutes of play. The 75,000 had paid R525,000 to watch the match which was over £300,000, but the temporary seats did not please visiting British supporters; it positively alarmed them, and the Transvaal Rugby Union, with its great wealth, must make a decision soon or there could be another 'Pretoria' disaster. There is no doubt that Loftus Versveld, Kings Park, and Boet Erasmus were the best grounds, while

Bloemfontein was big, but rather too vast an arena for good viewing.

The Lions were penalised on going down at a scrum after five minutes and Jackie Snyman kicked a splendid goal from 45 yards. Then Windsor was hurt with a badly cut forehead but refused to come off, preferring to play with his head heavily bandaged. His injury was closely followed by one to McLauchlan who suffered deep bruising of the thigh and a 'shiner' and he, too, insisted on remaining on the field. Only the player knows whether or not he is fit enough to continue, and both said they wanted to continue, and yet one feels they were not one hundred per cent, and could have given way to replacements, even though this would have hurt their pride, for they had both played so well on tour. However, the injuries were not simple ones, and both proved painful, but these two Lions were 'hard' men and Mighty Mouse had already played for Scotland with a fractured leg.

Although the Lions were to take the lead after 10 minutes it soon became obvious that this was a different test from the previous three, as the Springboks were doing so much better at forward and winning good possession at the line-out where John Williams was jumping high and feeding Bayvel, who at scrum-half was rather nervous, hesitant, and untidy with his service. However, the Lions were getting little ball from the line-out and finding the Springboks ready to wheel the scrum on the Lions put in, to make the delivery to Edwards untidy. Obviously, the Springboks had given much thought after the third test to ways and means of denying the Lions good possession and of winning better ball themselves.

The Lions first try after 10 minutes came from a Springbok heel outside their own goal line and this time the Lions wheeled and the ball shot past Bayvel for flanker Uttley and wing Pope to dive for it. Both believe they got there first and the try was awarded to Uttley although from the Press Box one could not be sure and even pictures do not always reveal what happened and strangely enough, in this vital test there were three 'doubtful' tries, two allowed and one not, and only one really good one, the second for the Lions by Irvine. Max Baise was not quite at his best as a referee, on the day, because things did not 'run' for him and he was often out of position while he did stand, far too frequently, on the Lions side of the line-out. One believes he had been 'chivvied' in the morning by friends who suggested that Gareth Edwards had 'talked' Cas de Bruyn through the Third Test as Colin Meads used to do but, anyway, Max Baise was not as happy in this match as normally.

Bennett converted Uttley's try and it was 6–3 but after 25 minutes of rather scrappy play and several missed kicks at goal; one by Irvine from 48 yards, two by Snyman from 50 and 38 yards respectively, and a low drop at goal by Cronje, the Springboks drew level when the Lions were trapped inside the 10 yards mark at a line-out and Snyman kicked a neat goal from the '25' line to make it 6–6. Play continued to be hard and searching but not as free or as skilful, at least by the Lions, until the interval approached and, as was their habit during the tour, the Lions moved into the lead, with a good try, the only really clean and decisive one of the match, and engineered by the 'old master', Edwards.

The Lions won a scrum 15 yards out from the Springbok line and held it with a blindside of 10 yards on the right. Then they released the ball, Davies to Edwards, and away shot the scrum-half to the blindside, drawing in the wing and the full-back towards him, and this left the way clear for Irvine, cracking on the pace. Edwards timed his pass perfectly and Irvine crossed the line but moved in ten yards towards the posts. Unfortunately, through his injured knee, Bennett was not kicking with his usual accuracy and his conversion attempt sailed wide. As things were shaping these two points would have been valuable, but neither Bennett nor Irvine were kicking well on the day, following their magnificent accuracy in other matches. It was just one of those days for most of the Lions.

Before the interval Snyman kicked wide from 25 yards and so the Springboks 'gunners' were just as inaccurate as their opponents. At half time the Lions were 10–6 in the lead but the match was a far from being decided. I had an 'open' telephone line to Cardiff and the result would soon 'hit the street', as the say in New Zealand. Yet one appreciated that the Lions would have to make a special effort in the second half if they were to put themselves out of range of defeat. Yet although they tried hard to do so, the course of events proved far different from what we had anticipated and certainly more exciting. It was to be a 'cliff hanger' and, as McBride said, 'another test of character'.

Bennett and Irvine missed with penalty attempts in the first five minutes of the second half, that would have put the Lions ten points clear and, possibly, out of trouble but the growing Springboks effort brought them level mid-way through the half, to set the match alight. The Springboks moved away to their right, just inside the Lions half. Schlebusch slipped through and sent right-wing Pope racing round J. J. Williams. Up the touch line he went, before J. P. R. Williams cracked him down where he sent the ball inside before Williams and he fell into touch. One sensed that Schlebusch made a grab at the loose rolling ball and knocked on, before Cronje raced up to gather and dive over for a try. Referee Baise was alongside Cronje and signalled a try – the first by the Springboks in the series – and both players and spectators in the vicinity jumped high. It was for them a 'miracle', as the mighty Lions goal line had been crossed after 3½ matches of effort. Snyman's conversion attempt was just wide and so it was 10–10, and one could feel the crowd lifting itself for a great finish. Ten minutes later the Springboks were in the lead!

Referee Baise suddenly turned round at a line-out and caught the Lions midfield players inside the ten yards line, just inside the Lions '25' area, and Snyman came up to take the kick. He made no mistake and as the Springboks sailed into the lead, the temporary stands rattled. The scent of victory was in the air. The Lions were being mauled and if the Springboks could win it would be an historic victory but, suddenly, the serious nature of the occasion hit the Lions. McLauchlan trotted up with McBride for the restart and was seen to chat to his captain and pat him on the back. No doubt he said, 'We can do it, Willie!'

They girded their loins for the big effort, and after 36 minutes they levelled the scores again, much to the relief of camp followers, not least myself. It was the shrewd Edwards that engineered the score by doing his 'disappearing act' from a set scrum on the Springboks '25', well to the left of the posts. Full-back Roux came up to stop him and fell offside for referee Baise to award the kick, which we believed to be the last chance for the Lions to save the match.

Irvine did not fail this time, and the ball sailed high between the posts although, for some unknown reason, one of the touch judges did not raise his flag. It was a goal, an invaluable one, even more valuable for the Lions than Irvine's superb goal against

England in the last match at Murrayfield. Now the Springboks were in danger as the Lions raised their game for a final effort to win the match, and they did try, really hard, and thought they did win it!

However, before their special effort, Jackie Snyman made the best run of the match, behind the scrum, when he set off up the middle of the field to turn the defence, and then moved to his left where Muller was unmarked on the left wing with 30 yards to go. The pass was made; alas, for South Africa, Muller dropped it, but may not have got to the corner, even if it was a wonderful chance of winning the match. Back came the Lions to the other end and J. P. R. Williams joined the line to thrust through, before turning inside and linking up with Slattery in the Springboks '25'. Off went the Irish flanker, charging and diving, as defenders met him on the goal line. It was Cronje who fell underneath him but Slattery pressed the ball down between the centre's legs and claimed he scored. One expected referee Baise to raise his hand for a try . . . the winning try!

But no, he stepped out to order a five yard scrum. Why? It should have been a try or a drop-out. Cronje told Slattery that he believed he had scored. Later there were pictures to suggest it was a fair try, as there were pictures to indicate the doubt concerning Uttley's try. As one paper suggested, 'Pictures Pin-point Baise "blues" ' and it was just not his day. The Lions won the five yard scrum for Edwards to feed J. J. Williams on the blind side, and he was nearly over for his 13th try. He was held up, the whistle went, and referee Baise raced away to the tunnel with Lions in pursuit and asking questions.

It was all over! The Grand Tour was over. The Lions were unbeaten and the Springboks had avoided a fourth and final defeat. A draw was a fair result, taking the match as a whole, but the Lions could have won it. They did not play as well as they should have done and in the second half, the strain of the long tour revealed itself, among the forwards, and the backs lacked their normal sharpness. Gareth Edwards and J. P. R. Williams were game competitors until the end; that is their attitude to rugby, as there is always hope until the final whistle is blown.,

As the crowd dispersed a rescue helicopter landed on Ellis Park to take away a spectator suffering from a heart attack. One man had died in the stands; four others were taken ill. It was that kind of match. An exciting cliff-hanger in the second half, but not a match of great spectacle. There were too many errors by both sides. Each had the chance to clinch it, but the dying seconds of the game will be talked about for many a day, especially in Ireland.

Yet the Lions could walk tall. Unbeaten in 22 matches, and improving on the record of 1971. British rugby was at the top, at long last, and while there was a feeling of anti-climax about it all, one realised that in retrospect, the glory would be great for Alun Thomas and his party. The SA Board praised the Lions, management and players. They called them the 'Greatest'. They were! Mr Heath said he would come to Heathrow to greet the returning Lions and this gesture caused the Government to perform the 'about turn' act again and Denis Howell, as Minister of Sport, agreed to do the same. The Lions had conquered all – the Springboks; the anti-apartheid group, as young Peter Hain somersaulted; and the British Government which had disowned them on tour. They must be the 'Greatest'. If not, please tell me why?

Appendix 1

MATCH RECORDS OF 1974 LIONS

Played 22. Won 21. Drawn 1. Lost 0. Points for 729. Points against 207.

No.	Date	Opponents	Venue	Result	For				Against				For	Agst.	Attendances
					g	p	t	dg	g	p	t	dg			
1	May 15	Western Transvaal	Potchefstroom	Won	7	3	2	–	1	1	1	–	59	13	25,000
2	May 18	South West Africa	Windhoek	Won	1	3	2	–	1	2	1	–	23	16	12,000
3	May 22	Boland	Wellington	Won	2	3	3	–	–	2	–	–	33	6	22,000
4	May 25	Eastern Province	Port Elizabeth	Won	2	4	1	–	1	–	2	–	28	14	30,000
5	May 29	S.W. Districts	Mossell Bay	Won	15	1	1	–	–	–	–	–	97	0	7,000
6	June 1	Western Province	Newlands	Won	–	3	2	–	–	–	2	–	17	8	45,000
7	June 4	Proteas	Goodwood C.T.	Won	1	5	4	–	–	1	–	1	37	6	20,000
8	June 8	SOUTH AFRICA (1)	Newlands	Won	–	3	–	1	–	–	–	1	12	3	42,700
9	June 11	Southern Universities	Newlands	Won	2	2	2	–	–	–	1	–	26	4	20,000
10	June 15	Transvaal	Ellis Park	Won	1	3	2	–	–	3	–	2	23	15	68,000
11	June 18	Rhodesia	Salisbury	Won	3	3	3	1	–	2	–	–	42	6	22,000
12	June 22	SOUTH AFRICA (2)	Pretoria	Won	1	1	4	1	–	2	–	1	28	9	63,000
13	June 27	Quaggas	Ellis Park	Won	1	2	2	–	–	4	1	–	20	16	51,000
14	June 29	Orange Free State	Bloemfontein	Won	–	1	2	–	–	2	–	1	11	9	60,000
15	July 3	Griqualand West	Kimberley	Won	9	1	3	–	1	2	1	–	69	16	8,000
16	July 6	North Transvaal	Loftus Versveld	Won	1	2	1	–	–	4	–	–	16	12	55,000
17	July 9	African Leopards	East London	Won	5	2	5	–	–	2	1	–	56	10	15,000
18	July 13	SOUTH AFRICA (3)	Port Elizabeth	Won	1	2	2	2	–	3	–	–	26	9	55,000
19	July 17	Border	East London	Won	1	4	2	–	–	2	–	–	26	6	15,000
20	July 20	Natal	Kings Park, Durban	Won	3	4	1	–	–	2	–	–	34	6	38,000
21	July 23	Eastern Transvaal	Springs	Won	2	3	3	–	–	2	1	–	33	10	25,000
22	July 27	SOUTH AFRICA (4)	Ellis Park	Draw	1	1	1	–	–	3	1	–	13	13	75,000
															778,700
													Total Paid		R3,500,000

INDIVIDUAL RECORDS OF 1974 LIONS

		1. Western Transvaal	2. South West Africa	3. Boland	4. Eastern Province	5. South Western Districts	6. Western Province	7. Coloureds	8. South Africa	9. Southern Universities	10. Transvaal	11. Rhodesia	12. South Africa	13. Quaggas	14. Orange Free State	15. Griqualand West	16. Northern Transvaal	17. Africans	18. South Africa	19. Border	20. Natal	21. Eastern Transvaal	22. South Africa	Total Games	Tests	Penalty Goals	Trys	Conversions	Dropped Goals	Total Points
A. R. IRVINE	S		1		1	1		1		1		1		1		1	1	1	1	1	S	1	1	15	2	29	5	26	1	156
J. P. R. WILLIAMS	W	1		1		S	1		1		1		1	S	1		1		1	S	1	C	1	15	4		3			12
T. O. GRACE	I			1		1		1		1	1	1		1		1		1		1		1		11			13			52
W. C. C. STEELE	S	1			1		1		1			1	1		1	1				1				9	2		7			28
J. J. WILLIAMS	W		1	1		6T		1	1		1		1		1		1		1		1		1	12	4		12			48
C. REES	W	1	1		1		1			1				1										6			3			12
G. W. EVANS	E		1		1	1		1		1		1			1	1								8			4			16
R. A. MILLIKEN	I		1	1		1		1	1		1		1		1	1	1		1		1		1	13	4		5			20
I. R. McGEECHAN	S	1		1			1		1			1	1	1	1		1	1	1	1		1	1	14	4		2		1	11
R. T. E. BERGIERS	W	1			1		1			1	1	1		1						1		1		9			2			8
A. G. B. OLD	E		1	1		37P		1																4		7	1	17		59
P. BENNETT	W	1			1		1		1	1	1		1					1	1		1		1	11	4	21	1	15	2	103
J. J. MOLONEY	I	1				1		1		1	1			1		1						1		8			3			12
G. O. EDWARDS	W	S	C	1	C		1		1			C	1		1		1	1	1	1	1		1	15	4		7		1	31
A. G. RIPLEY	E	1		1			1				1			1		1		1		1		1		9			5			20
T. M. DAVIES	W		1		1	1		1	1			1	1		1		1		1		1		1	12	4		5			20
A. NEARY	E	1		1			1			1	1			1			1				1			8			2			8
J. F. SLATTERY	I		1		1	1		C	1			1	1		1	C		1			1		1	12	4		6			24
S. A. McKINNEY	I				1	1	1					1			1			1		1		1		8		1				3
T. P. DAVID	W	1	1	1						1				1		1		1		1		1		9			5			20
C. W. RALSTON	E		1			1		1		1		1		1	1	1		1		1	1	1	1	13	1					
R. M. UTTLEY	E		1	S	1			1	1	1	1	1	1			1	1	S	1	1		1	1	16	4		2			8
W. J. McBRIDE CAPT.	I	C		C		C	C		C		C		C				C	C	C		C		C	13	4		1			4
G. L. BROWN	S	1		1	1		1	1	1	1	1		1	1			1		1					12	3		8			32
F. E. COTTON	E	S	1	1		1		1	1		1	1	1	C			1		1		1		1	14	4					
M. A. BURTON	E				1	1		1						1		1		1		1		1		8						
J. McLAUCHLAN	S	1	1		1		1		1	C	1		1		1		1		1		1		1	13	4					
A. B. CARMICHAEL	S	1		1			1			1		1			1	1		1		1		1		10						
K. W. KENNEDY	I		1			1		1		1		1		1		1		1		1		1		10			2			8
R. W. WINDSOR	W	1		1	1		1		1		1		1		1		1		1		1		1	12	4					
C. M. H. GIBSON	I	Replacement for A. G. B. Old												1		1	1	1		1	1	1		7			2	1		10

Appendix 2

THE BRITISH ISLES IN SOUTH AFRICA
1891–1974
(Tour Records)

W. E. MACLAGAN'S 1891 TEAM

	P.	W.	D.	L.	F.	A.
PROVINCIAL MATCHES ...	16	16	0	0	213	1*
TEST MATCHES...	3	3	0	0	11	0
FULL TOUR	19	19	0	0	224	1

* In 1891 the value of a try was one point.
Top Points Scorer: A. Rotherham, 81 points.
Top Try Scorer: R. L. Aston, 30 tries.

J. F. HAMMOND'S 1896 TEAM

	P.	W.	D.	L.	F.	A.
PROVINCIAL MATCHES ...	17	16	1	0	276	29
TEST MATCHES...	4	3	0	1	34	16
FULL TOUR	21	19	1	1	310	45

Top Points Scorer: J. F. Byrne, 127 points.
Top Try Scorer: L. Q. Bulger, 19 tries.

M. C. MORRISON'S 1903 TEAM

	P.	W.	D.	L.	F.	A.
PROVINCIAL MATCHES ...	19	11	1	7	221	120
TEST MATCHES...	3	0	2	1	10	18
FULL TOUR	22	11	3	8	231	138

Top Points Scorer: R. T. Skrimshire, 59 points.
Top Try Scorer: R. T. Skrimshire, 10 tries.

T. SMYTH'S 1910 TEAM

	P.	W.	D.	L.	F.	A.
PROVINCIAL MATCHES ...	21	12	3	6	267	198
TEST MATCHES...	3	1	0	2	23	38
FULL TOUR	24	13	3	8	290	236

Top Points Scorer: C. H. Pillman, 65 points.
Top Try Scorer: M. E. Neale, A. R. Foster, 9 tries each.

R. COVE-SMITH'S 1924 TEAM

	P.	W.	D.	L.	F.	A.
PROVINCIAL MATCHES ...	17	9	2	6	160	112
TEST MATCHES...	4	0	1	3	15	43
FULL TOUR	21	9	3	9	175	155

Top Points Scorer: A. T. Voyce, 37 points.
Top Try Scorer: W. Wallace, 9 tries.

S. WALKER'S 1938 TEAM

	P.	W.	D.	L.	F.	A.
PROVINCIAL MATCHES ...	20	16	0	4	371	211
TEST MATCHES...	3	1	0	2	36	61
FULL TOUR	23	17	0	6	407	272

Top Points Scorer: A. R. Taylor, 53 points.
Top Try Scorer: E. L. Jones, 10 tries.

R. H. THOMPSON'S 1955 TEAM

	P.	W.	D.	L.	F.	A.
PROVINCIAL MATCHES ...	20	16	1	3	369	196
TEST MATCHES...	4	2	0	2	49	75
FULL TOUR	24	18	1	5	418	271

Top Points Scorer: A. J. F. O'Reilly, 48 points.
Top Try Scorer: A. J. F. O'Reilly, 16 tries.

A. R. SMITH'S 1962 TEAM

	P.	W.	D.	L.	F.	A.
PROVINCIAL MATCHES ...	20	15	3	2	331	160
TEST MATCHES...	4	0	1	3	20	48
FULL TOUR	24	15	4	5	351	208

Top Points Scorer: J. G. Willcox, 67 points.
Top Try Scorer: A. R. Smith, 8 tries.

T. J. KIERNAN'S 1968 TEAM

	P.	W.	D.	L.	F.	A.
PROVINCIAL MATCHES ...	16	15	0	1	339	120
TEST MATCHES...	4	0	1	3	38	61
FULL TOUR	20	15	1	4	377	181

Top Points Scorer: R. Hillier, 104 points.
Top Try Scorers: G. O. Edwards and A. J. W. Hinshelwood, 6 tries each.

W. J. McBRIDE'S 1974 TEAM

	P.	W.	D.	L.	F.	A.
PROVINCIAL MATCHES ...	18	18	0	0	650	173
TEST MATCHES...	4	3	1	0	79	34
FULL TOUR	22	21	1	0	729	207

Top Points Scorer: A. R. Irvine, 156 points.
Top Try Scorers: T. O. Grace, 13 tries; J. J. Williams, 12 tries.

Appendix 3

New Records created by 1974 Lions in South Africa

1. 97–0 win agaist South West Districts biggest defeat of Provincial Union in South Africa by visiting touring team.
2. 37 points by A. G. B. Old against South West Districts most scored by member of touring team in South Africa.
3. Total of 16 tries in South West Districts match most scored by British Isles side in any match abroad.
4. Six tries by J. J. Williams are most by any Lion in South Africa and equalled record of D. J. Duckham in New Zealand in 1971.
5. Total of 729 points is most scored by British Isles side abroad.
6. Total 156 points by A. R. Irvine most scored by Lion in South Africa.
7. Total of 107 tries most scored by Lions side in South Africa.
8. Eight tries by Gordon Brown most scored by visiting forward in South Africa.
9. Brown's try in Third Test at Boet Erasmus 1,000th point against South Africa in international matches.
10. Record of 21 wins in succession longest ever run in South Africa by touring team.
11. Unbeaten record on long tour only third in history, following 1891 Lions and 1924 All Blacks.
12. Every back in Lions side scored try on tour.
13. Second test victory of Lions by 28–9 was biggest defeat suffered by Springboks in international match and largest total registered against them. Third Test 26–9 was next.
14. Lions tally of 79 points is highest scored against South Africa in test series.

15. J. J. Williams achieved record twice of being first player to score two tries in test against South Africa, at home in Second and Third Tests. His four tries in series is also a record.
16. Four dropped goals by Lions in series is record for or against South Africa.
17. Ten tries to one is highest ratio against South Africa in any test series.
18. Ration of 107 tries to 14 against best by Lions team this century.